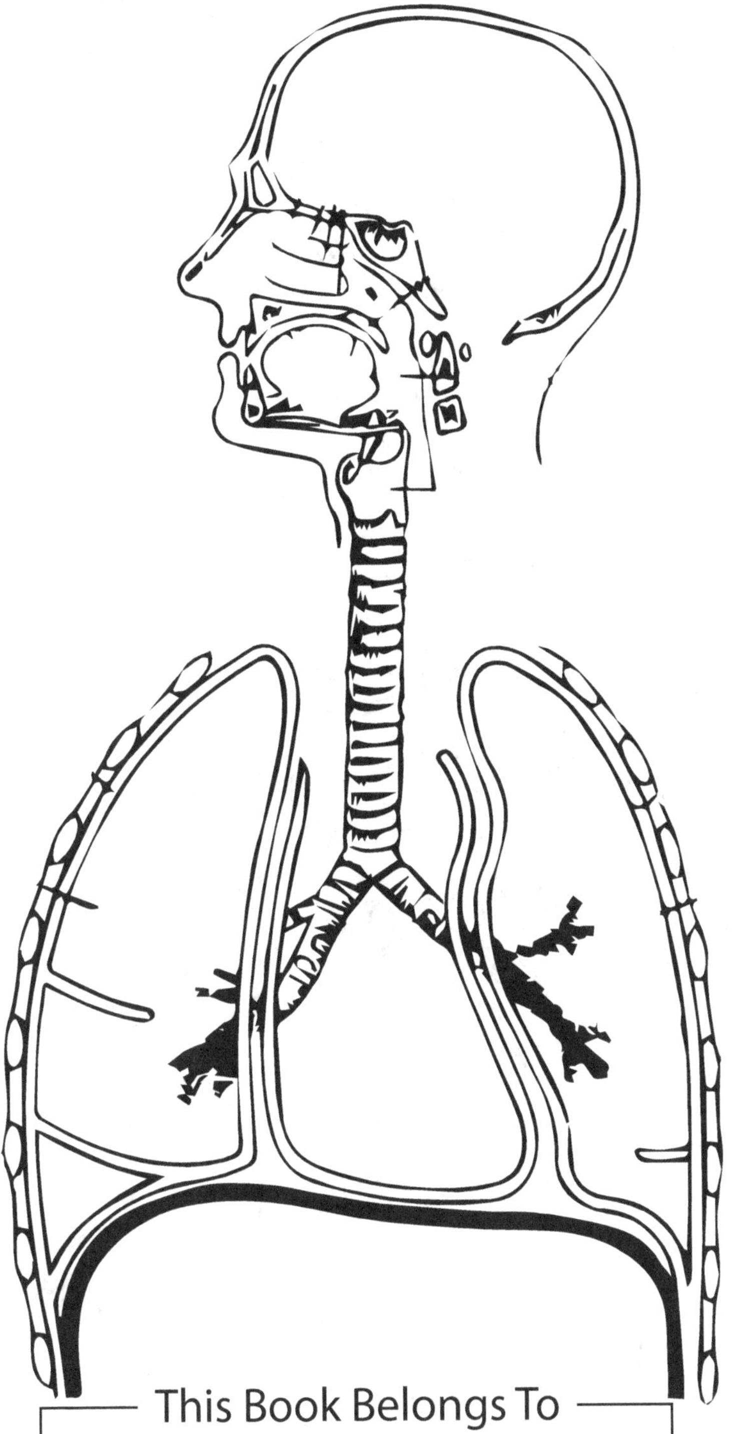

This Book Belongs To

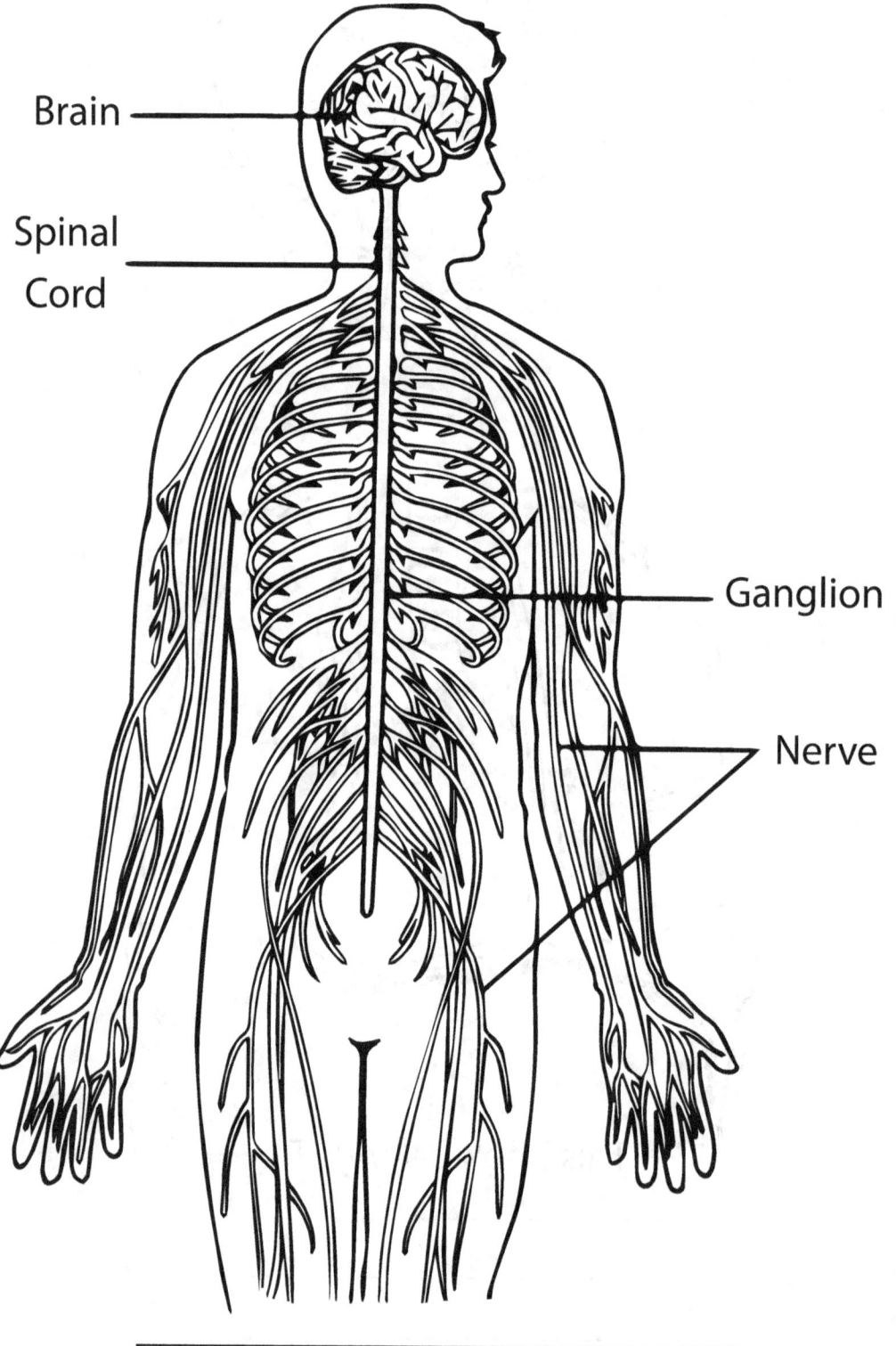

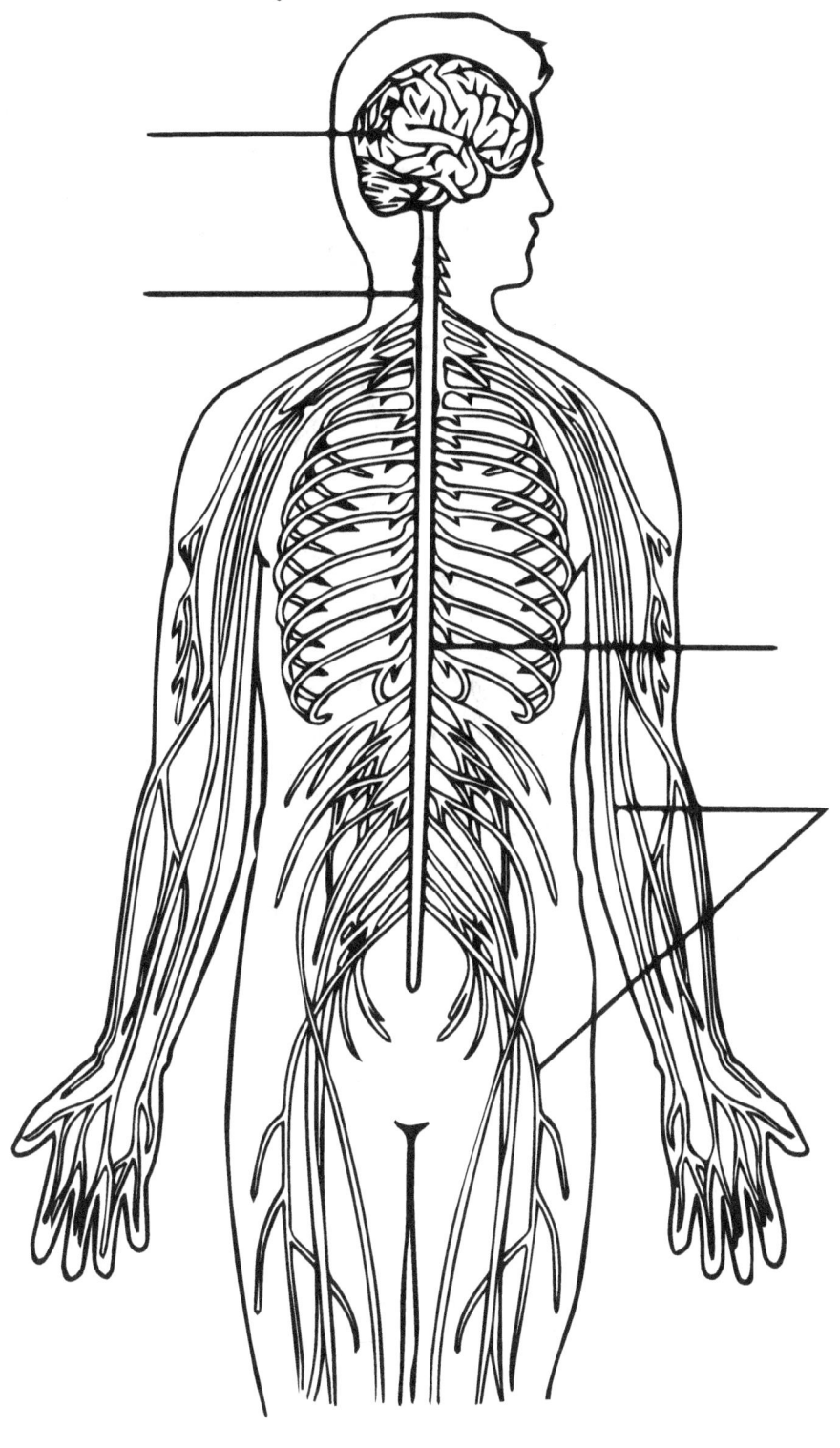

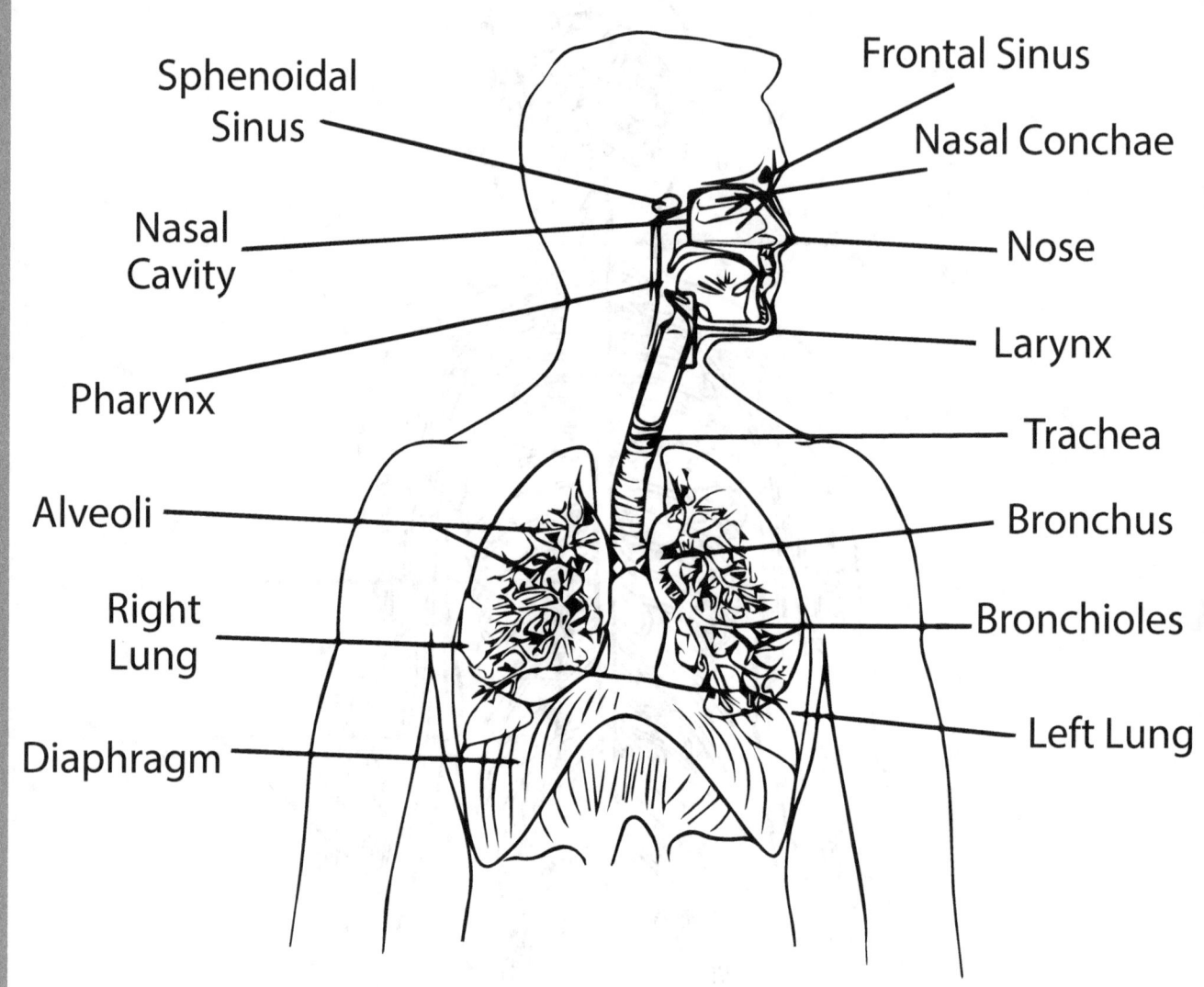

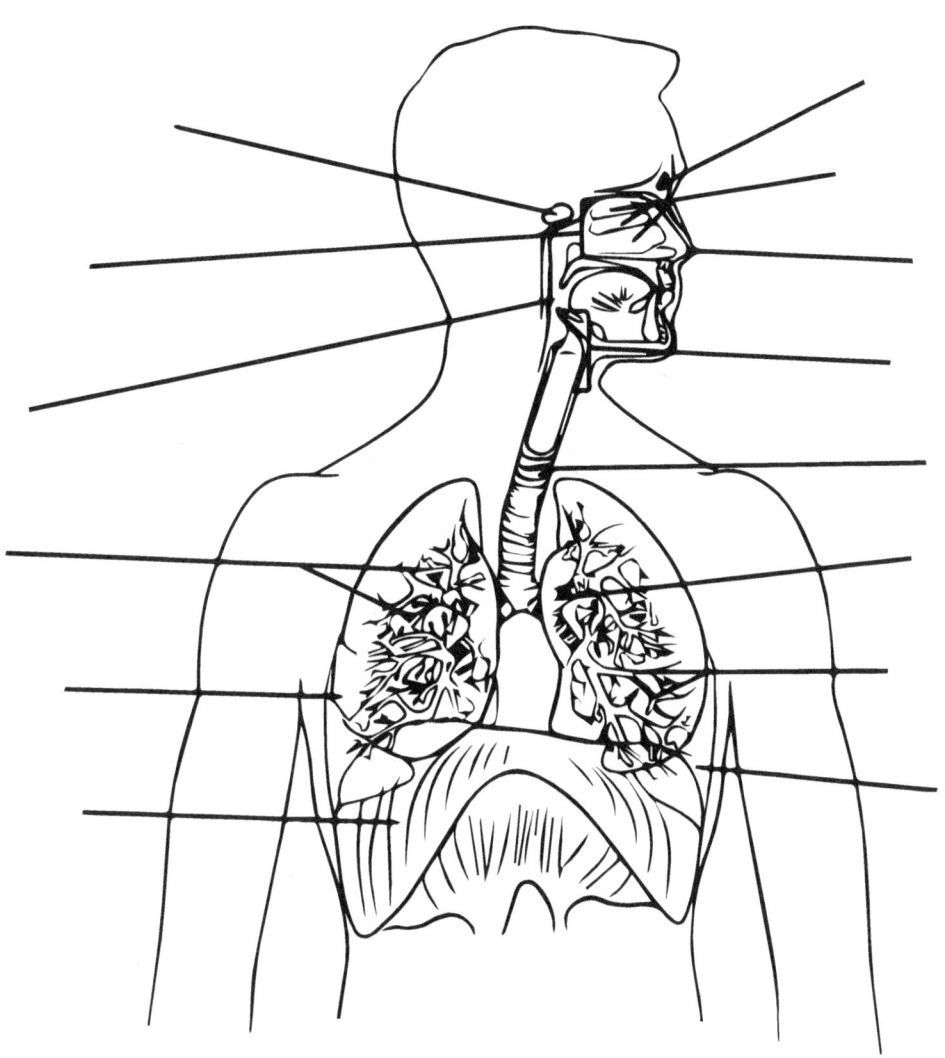

Respiratory System

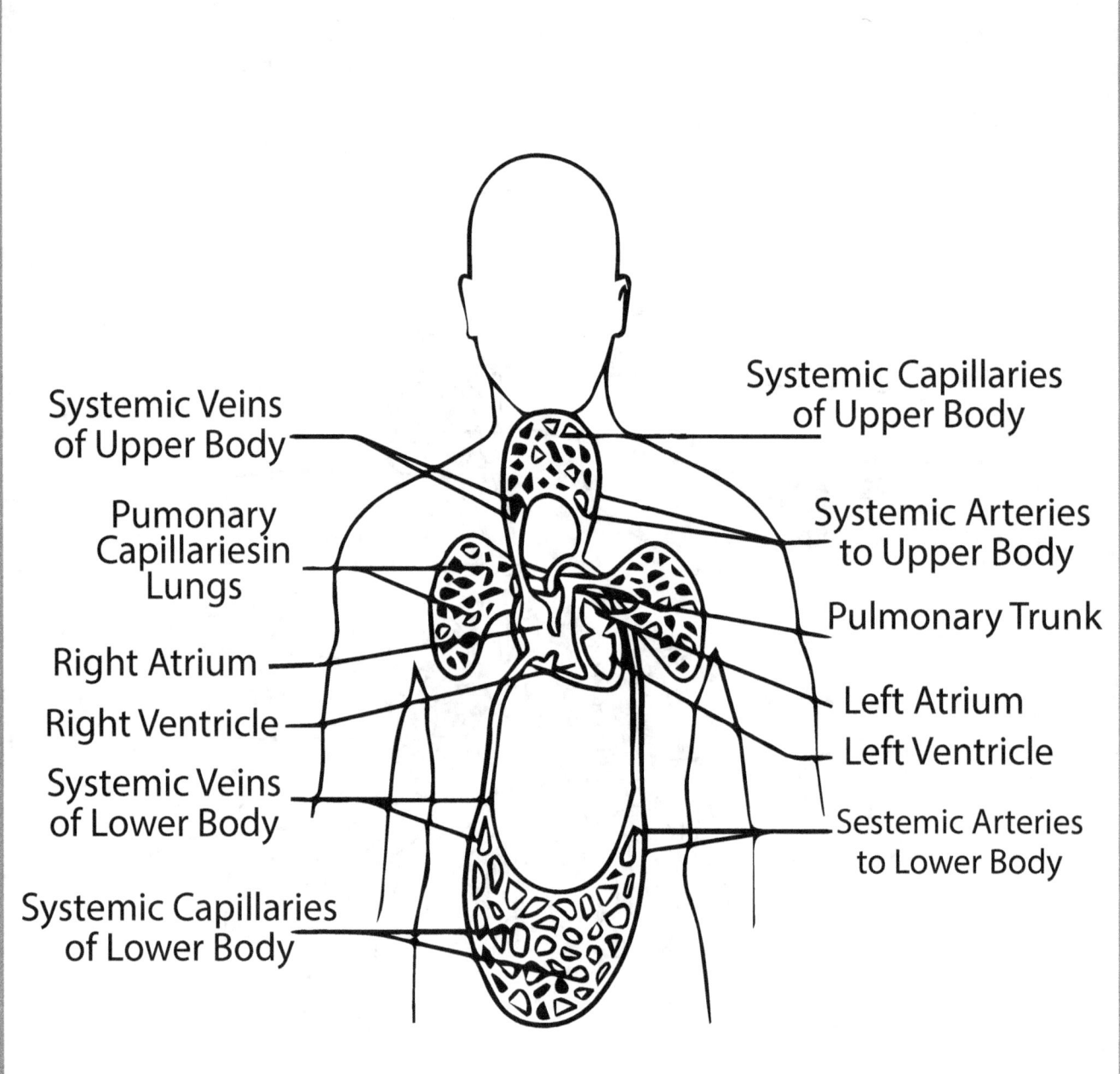

Human Circulatory System Part 1

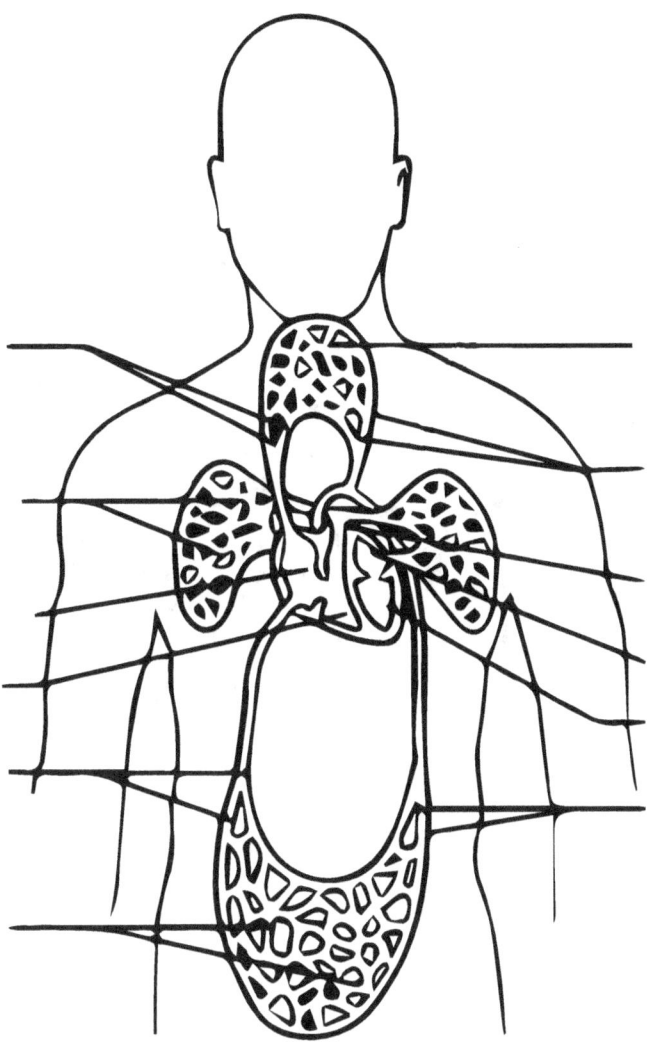

Human Circulatory System Part 1

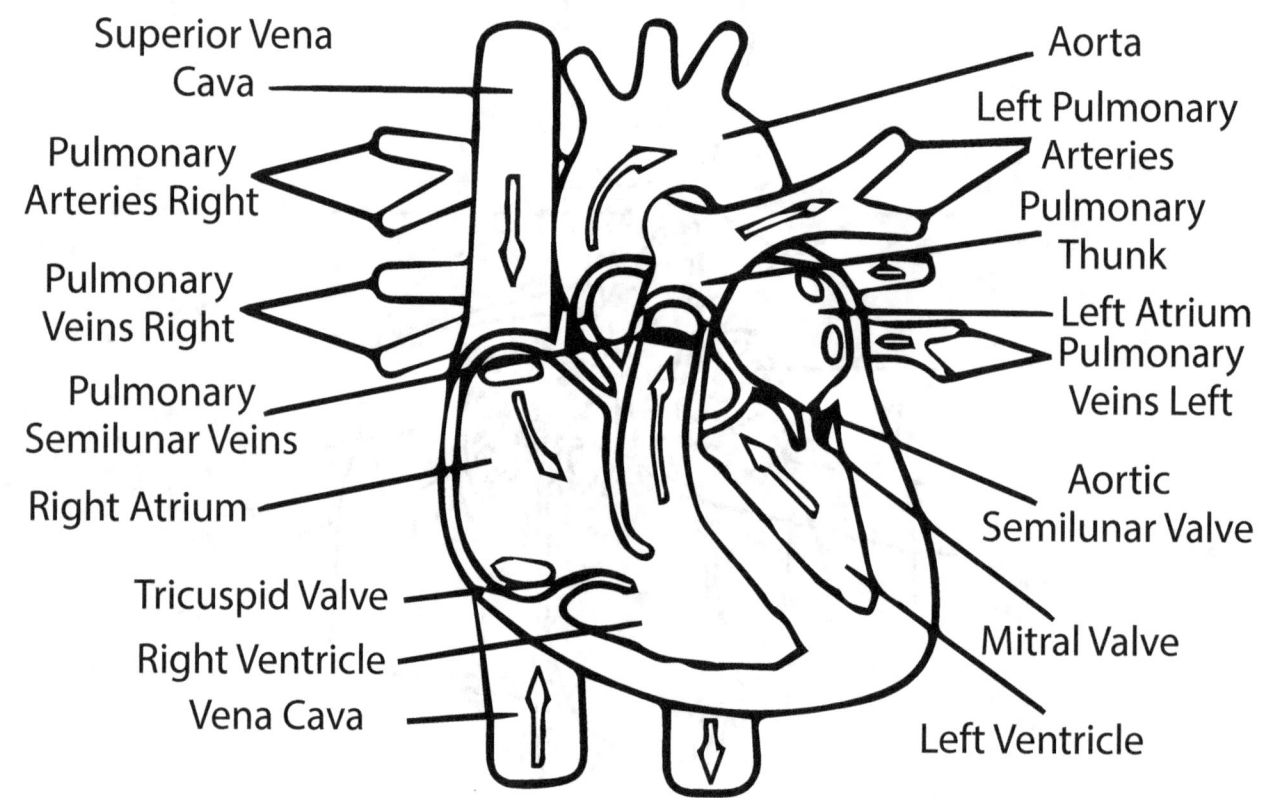

Human Circulatory System Part 2

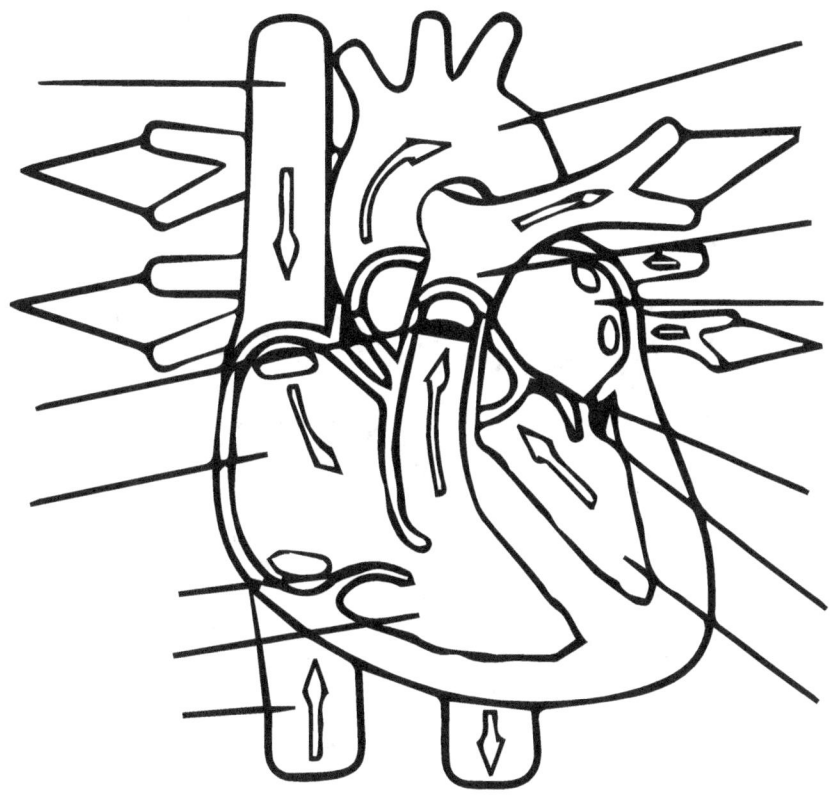

Human Circulatory System Part 2

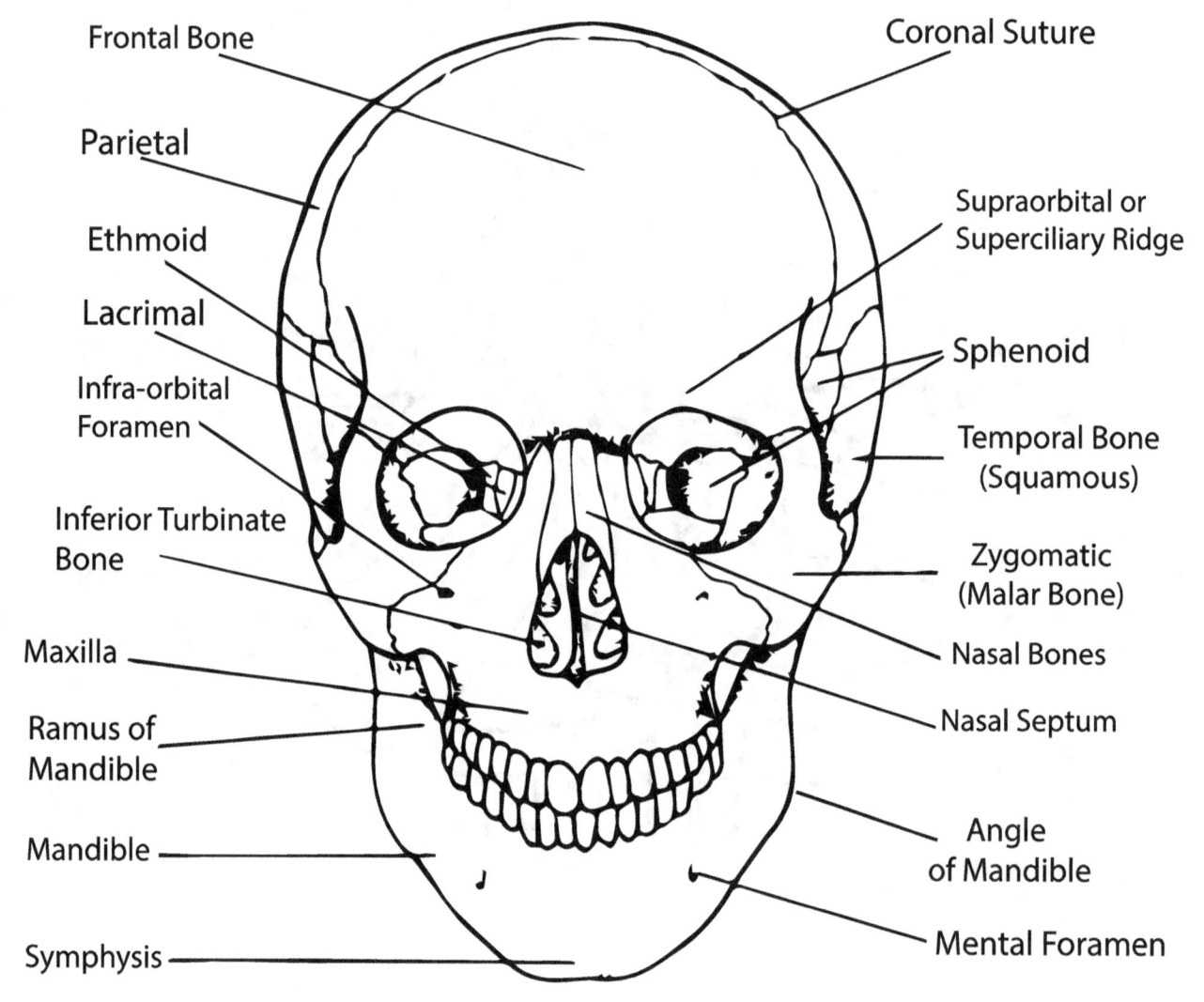

The Skull

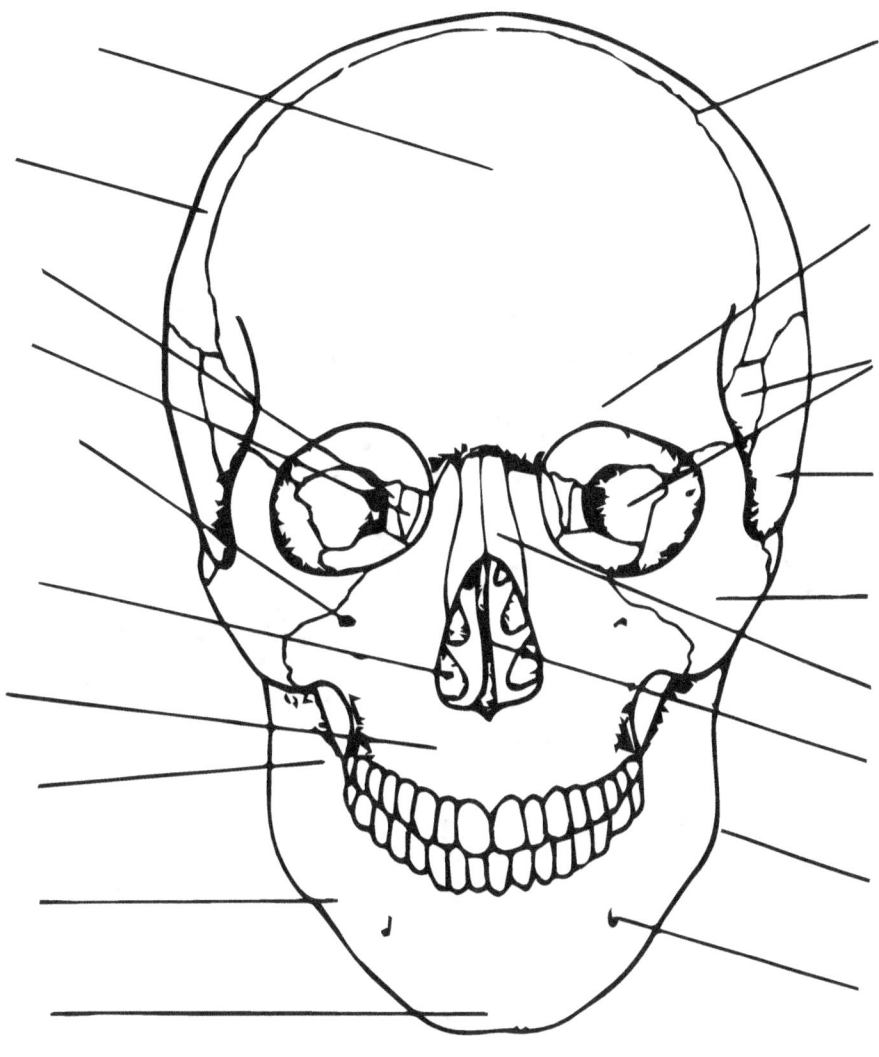

The Skull

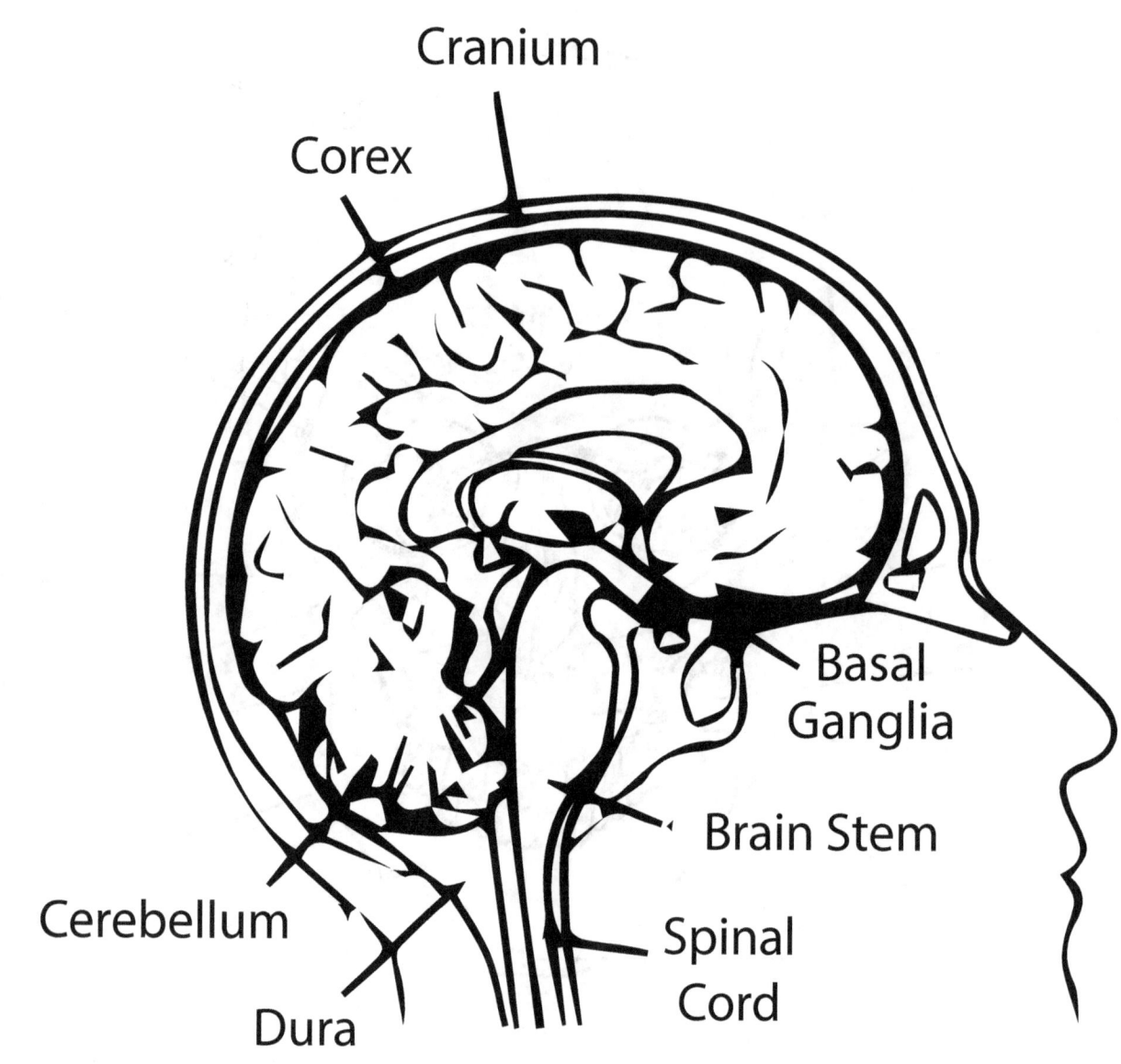

Human Brain Part 1

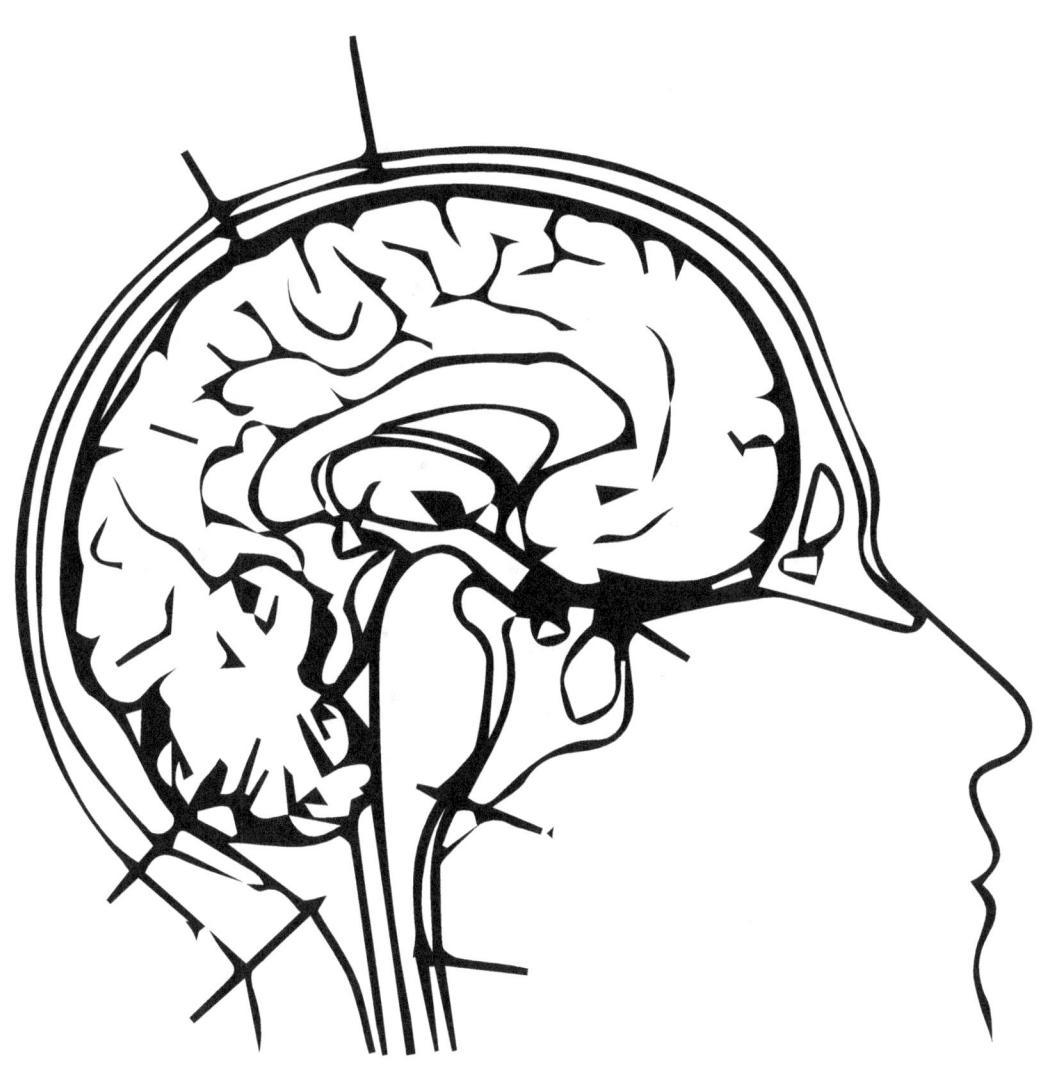

Human Brain Part 1

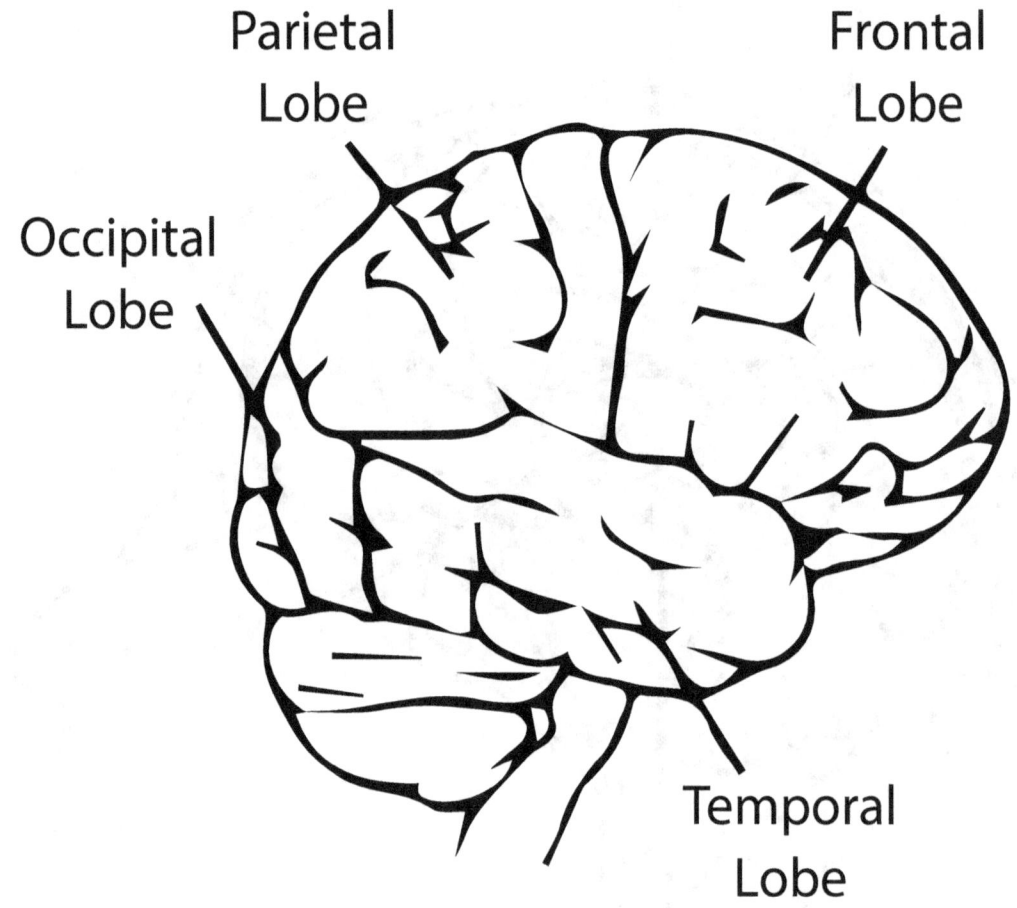

Human Brain Part 2

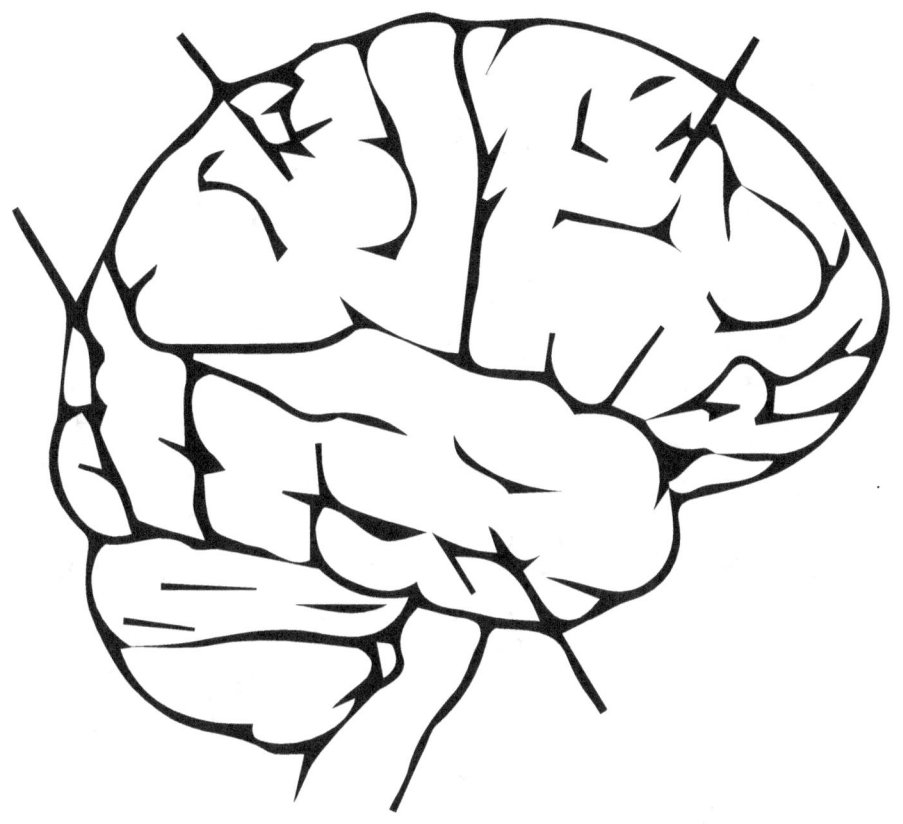

Human Brain Part 2

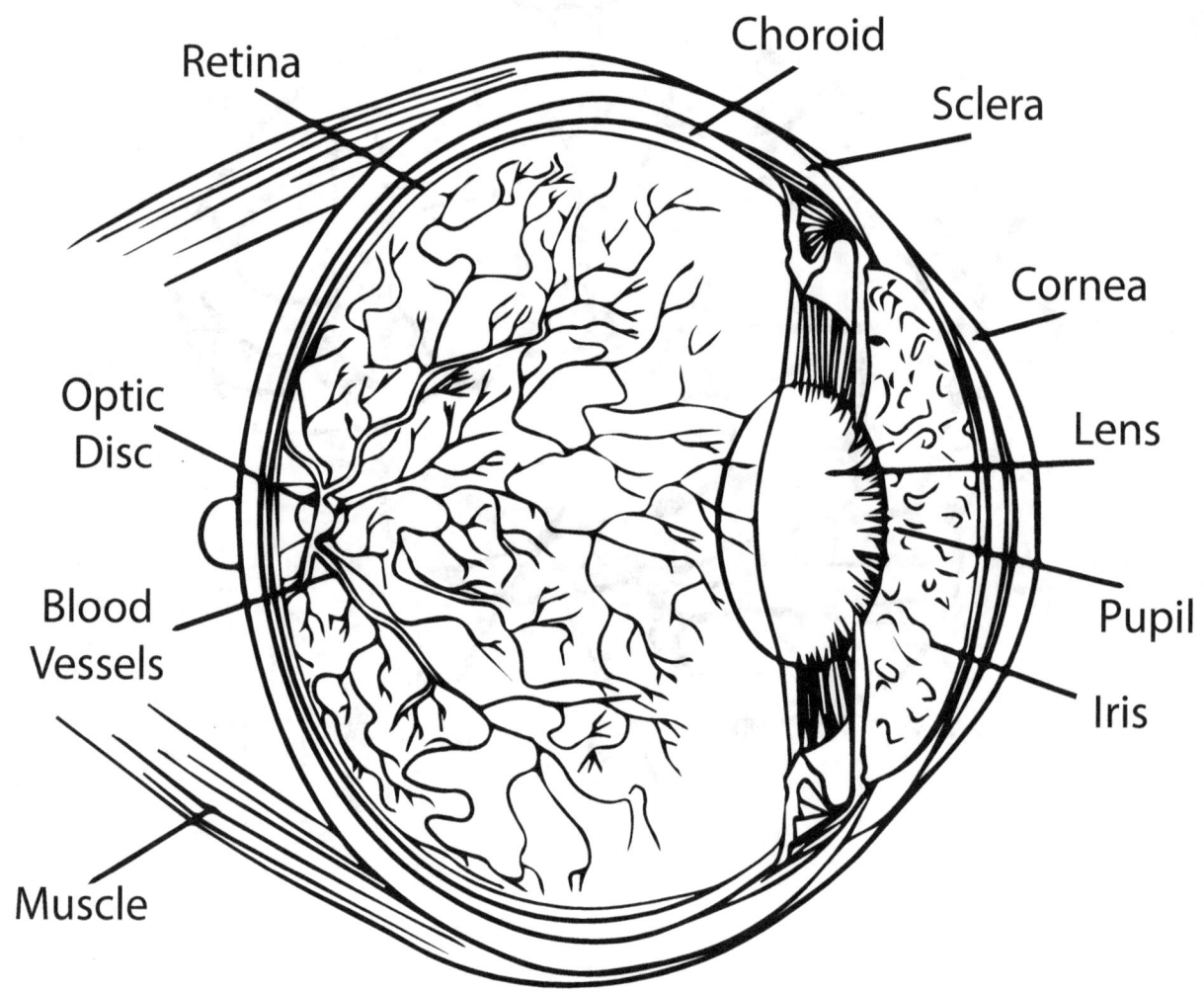

Anatomy Of The Eye

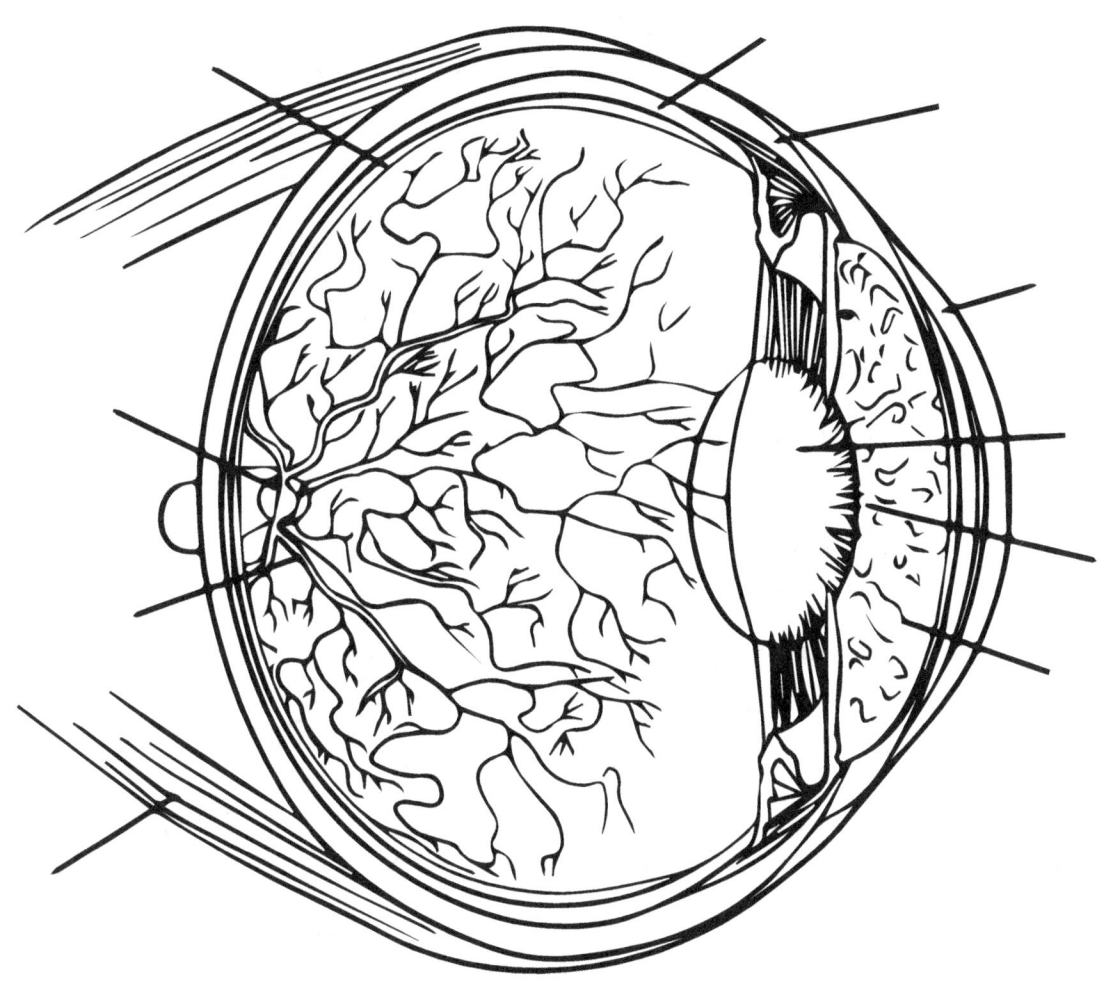

Anatomy Of The Eye

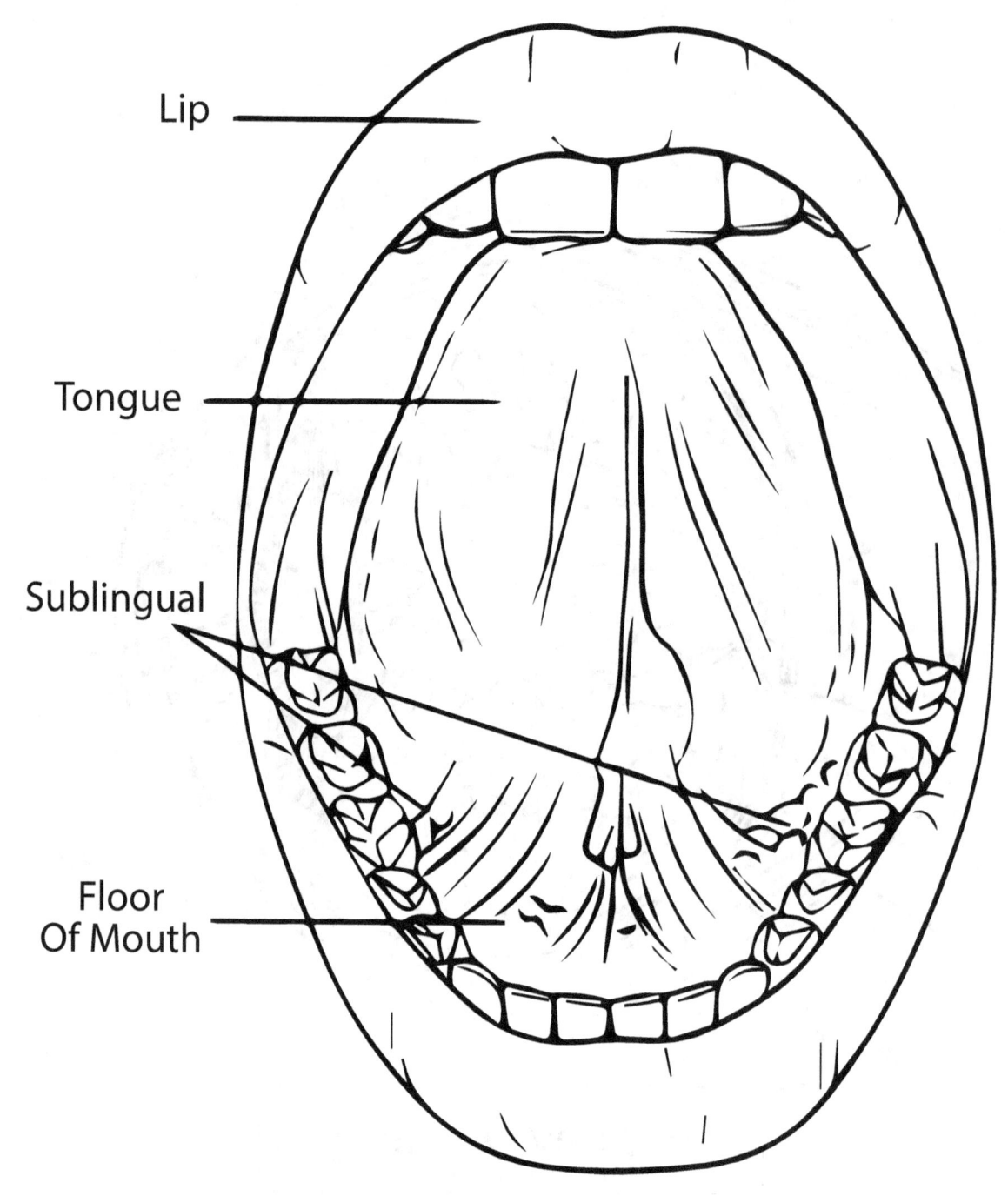

Mouth and Tongue

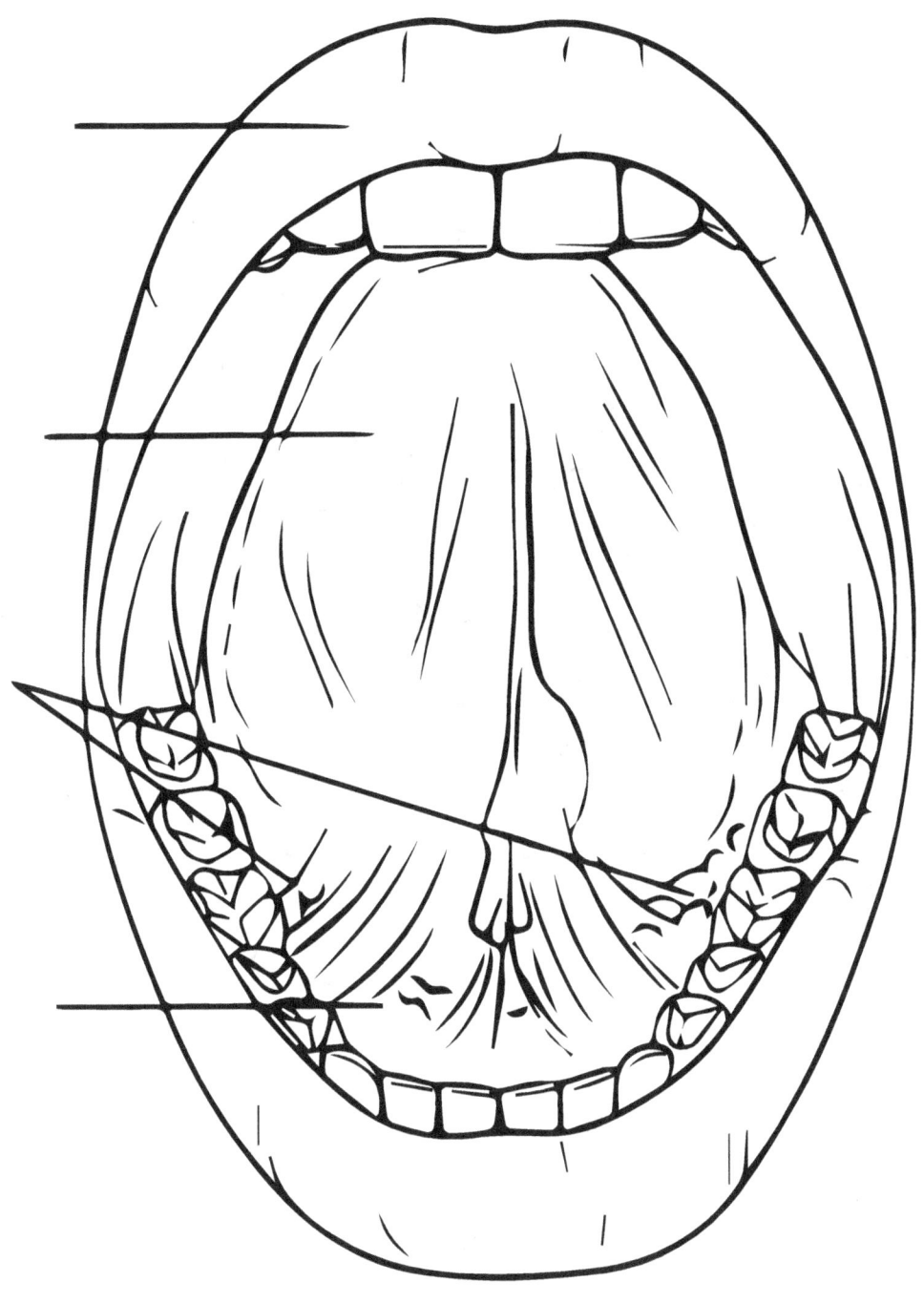

Mouth and Tongue

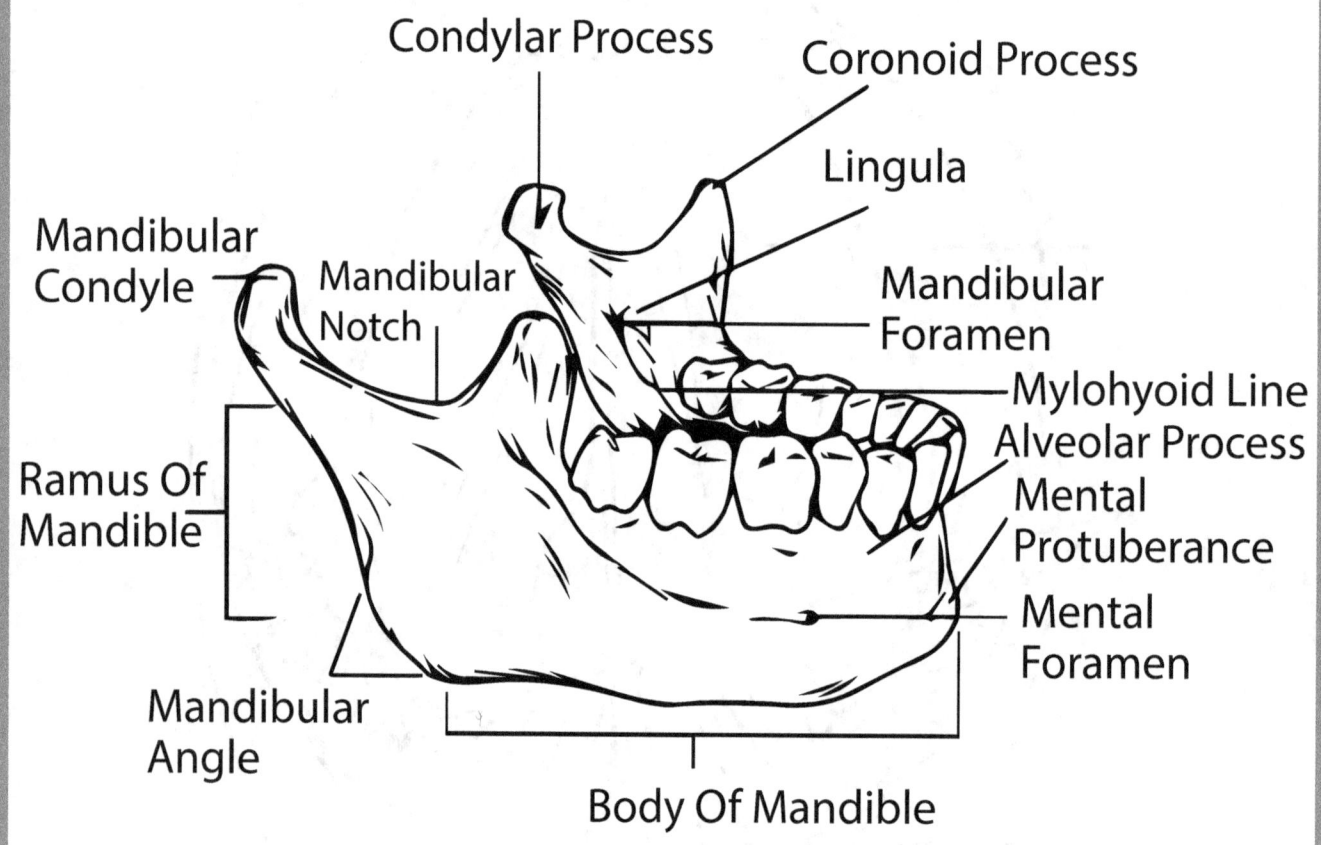

Right Lateral View

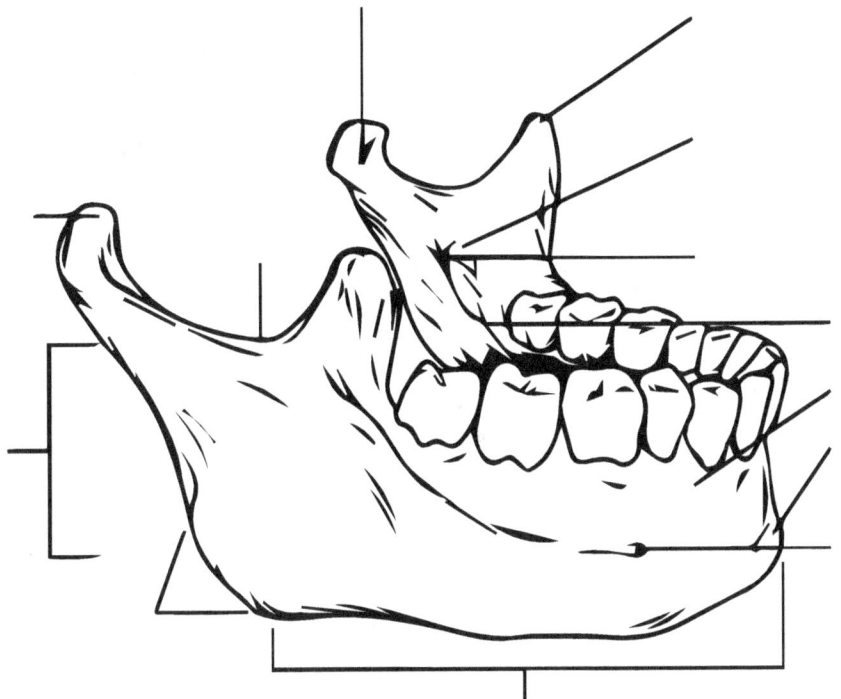

Right Lateral View

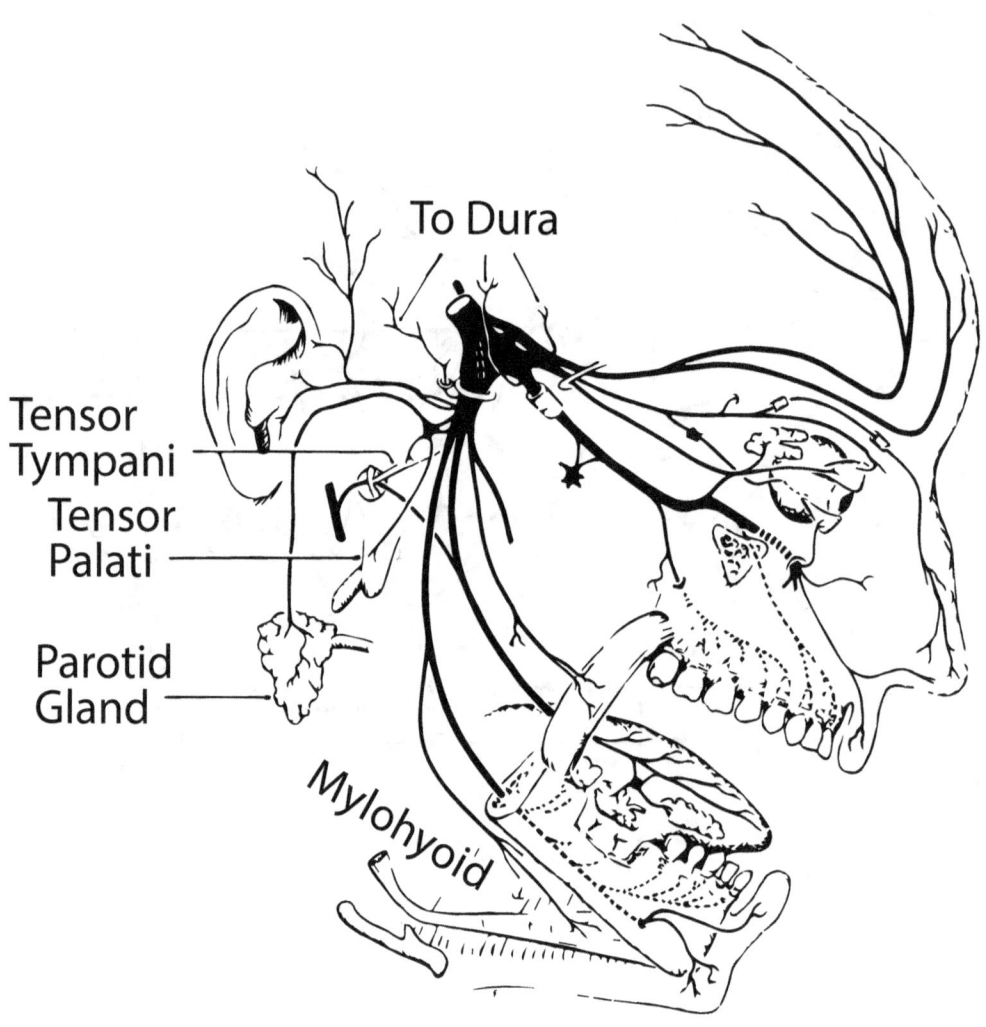

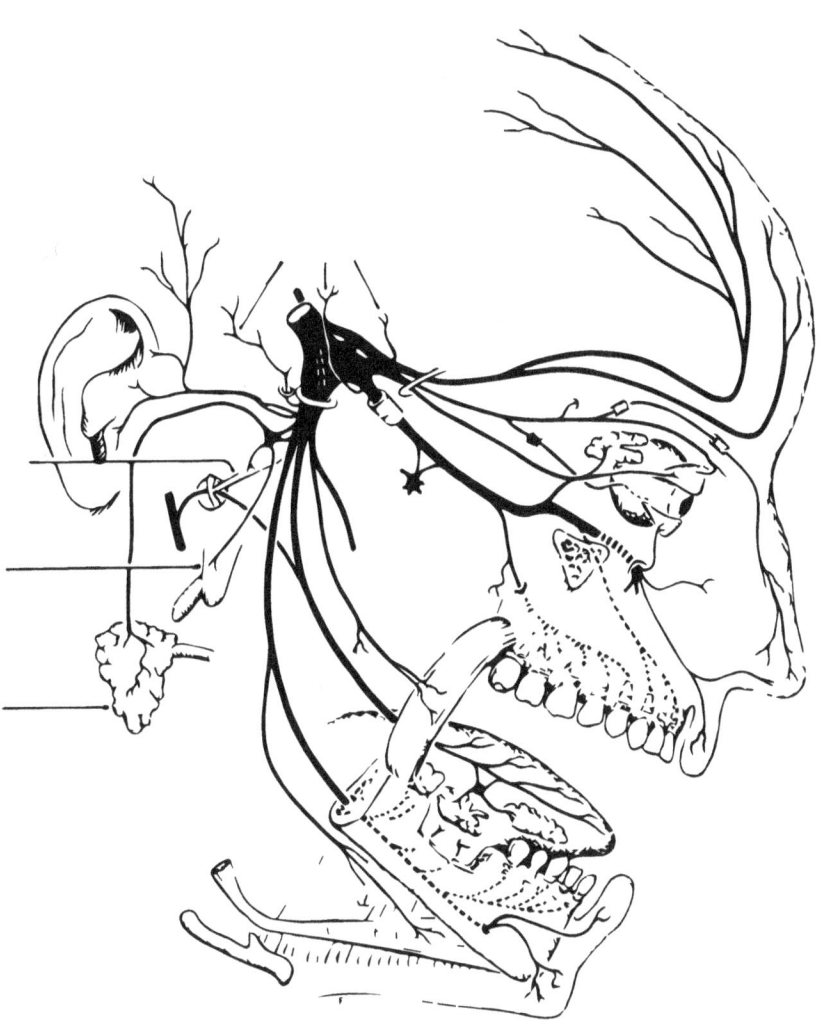

The Nerve V

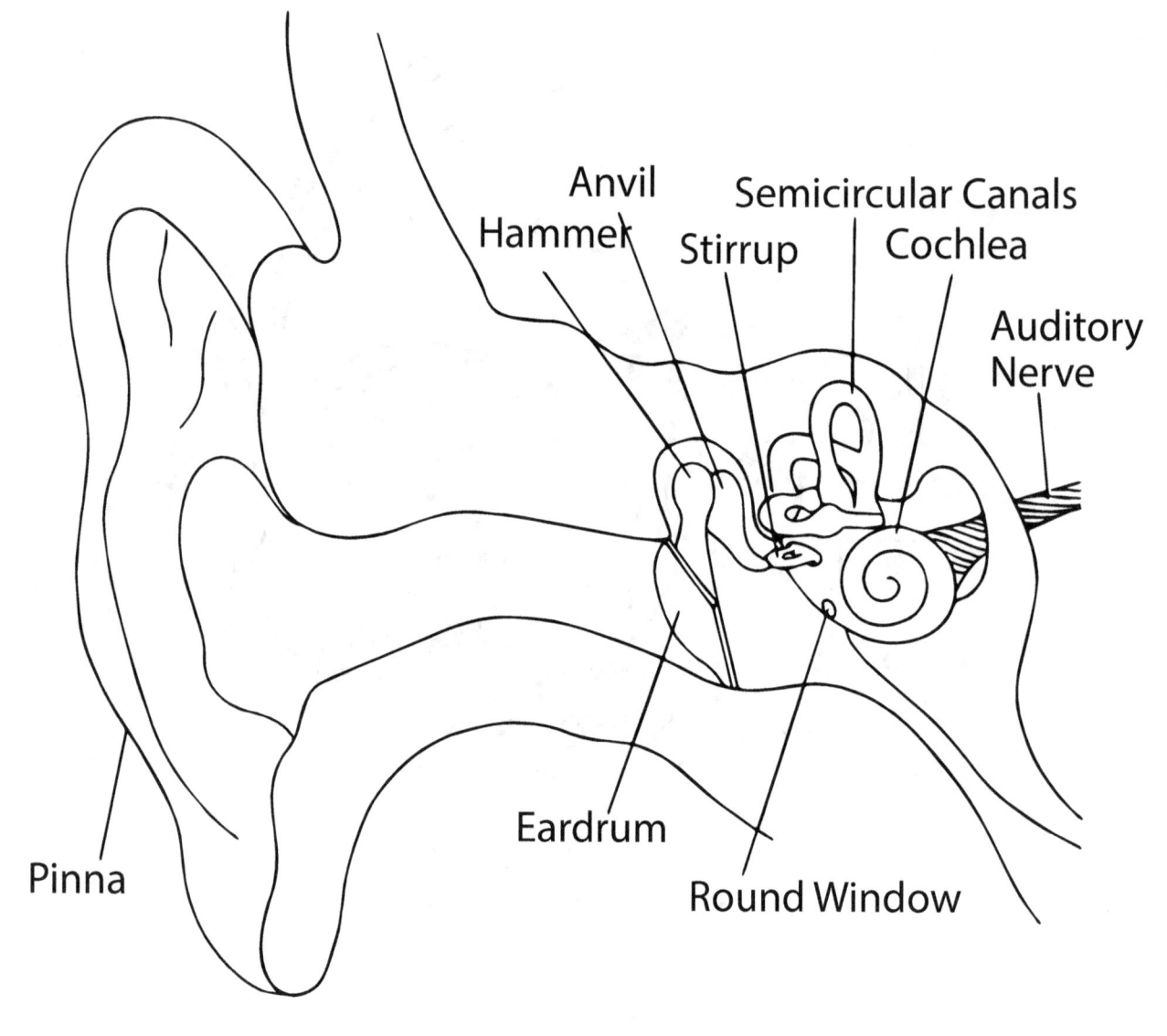

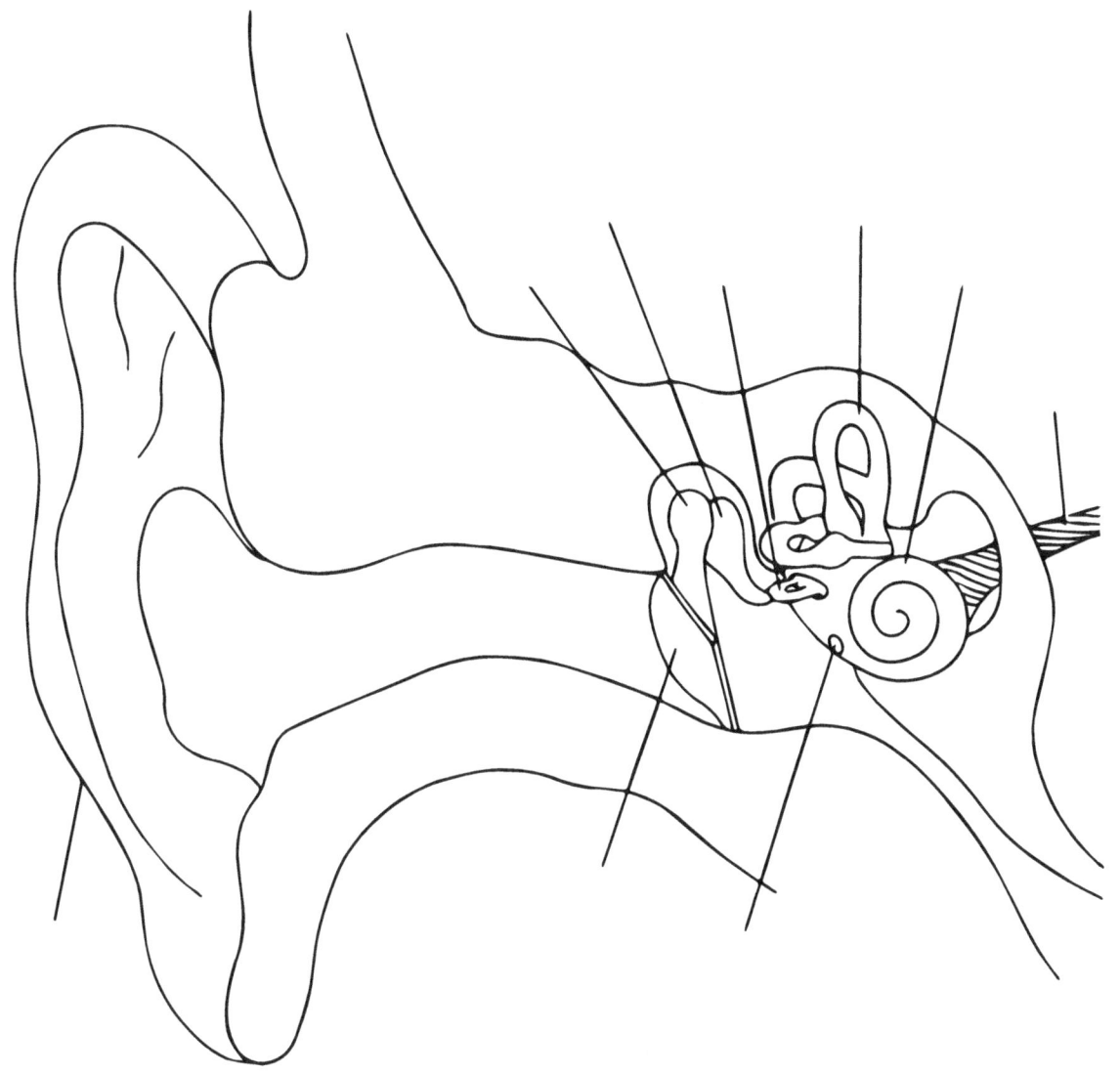

The Ear

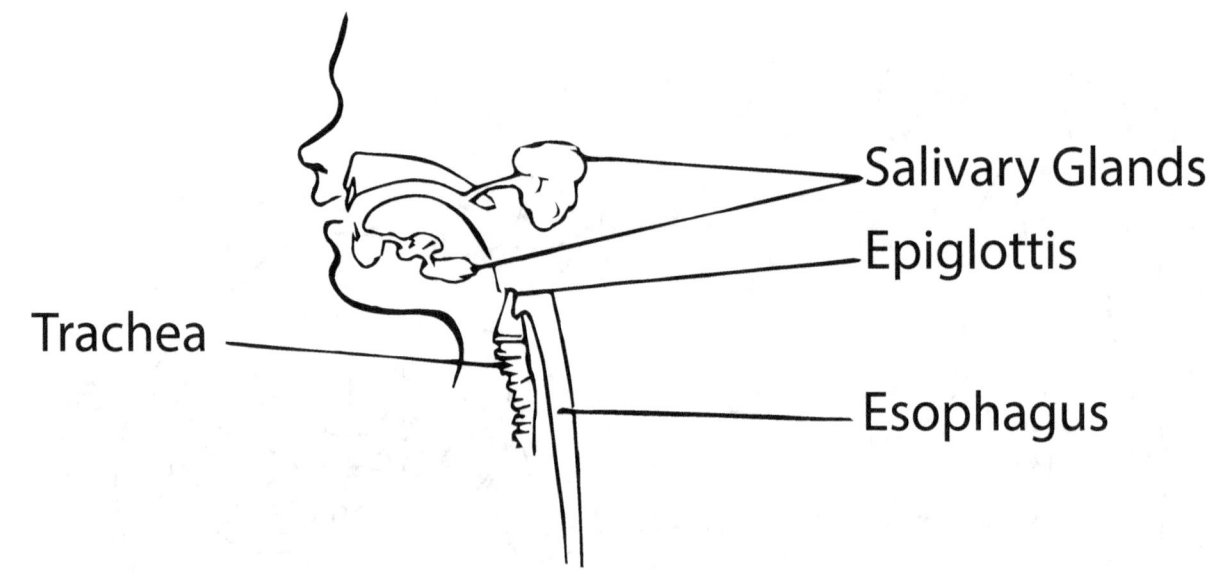

Trachea Respiratory System

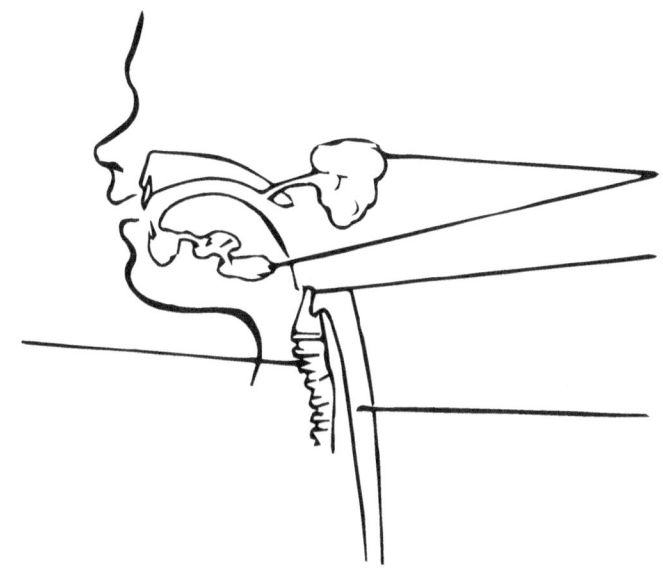

Trachea Respiratory System

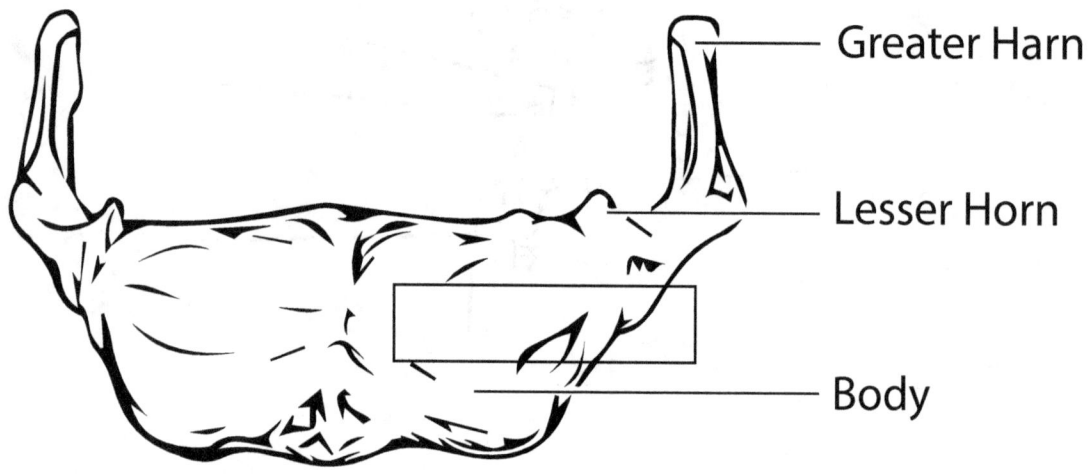

Lateral view

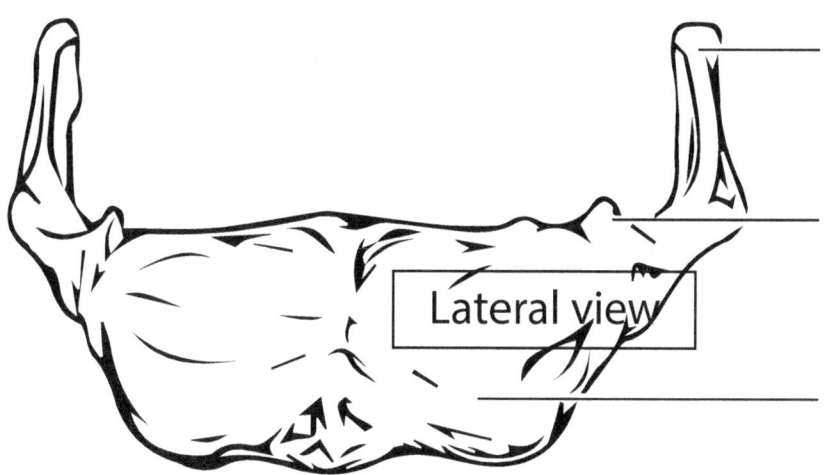

Lateral view

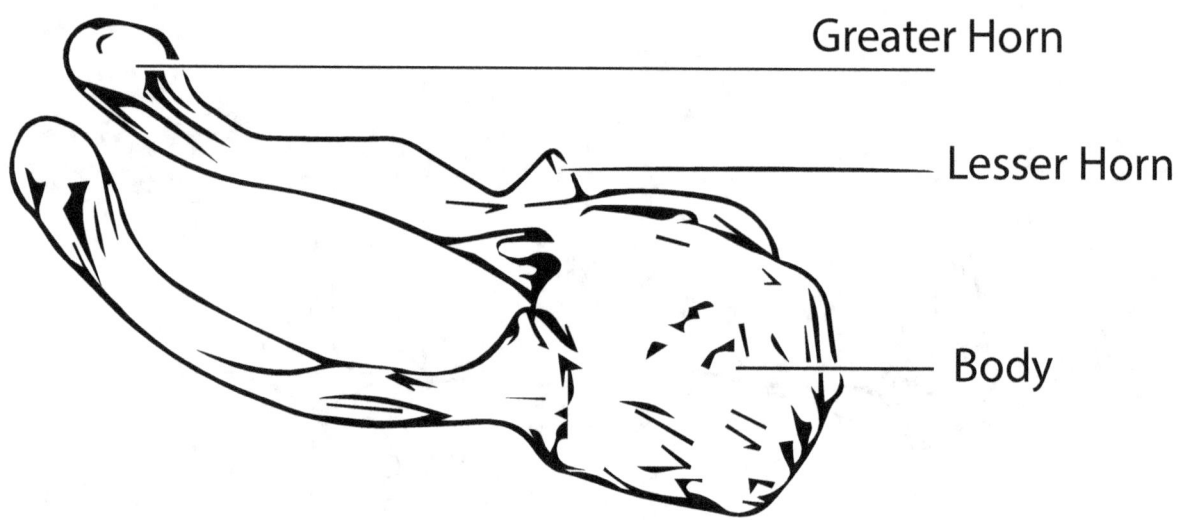

Right Lateral view

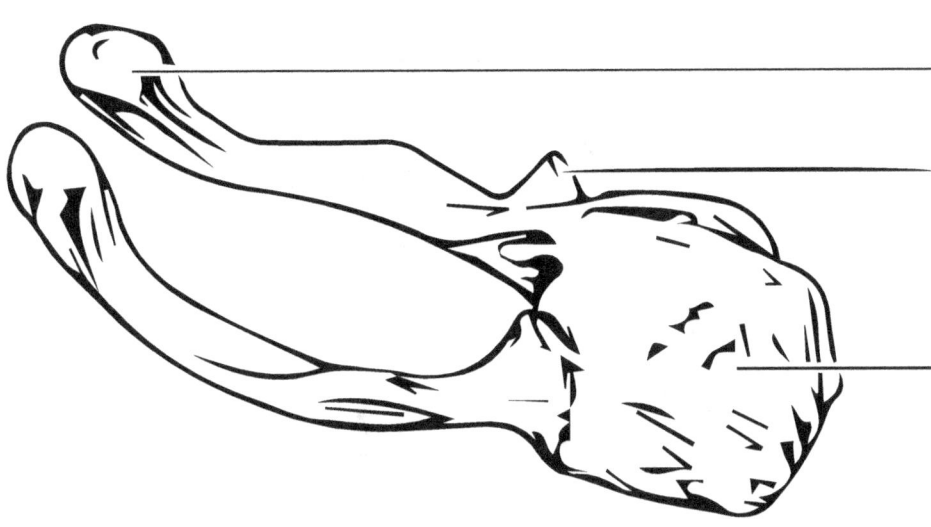

Right Lateral view

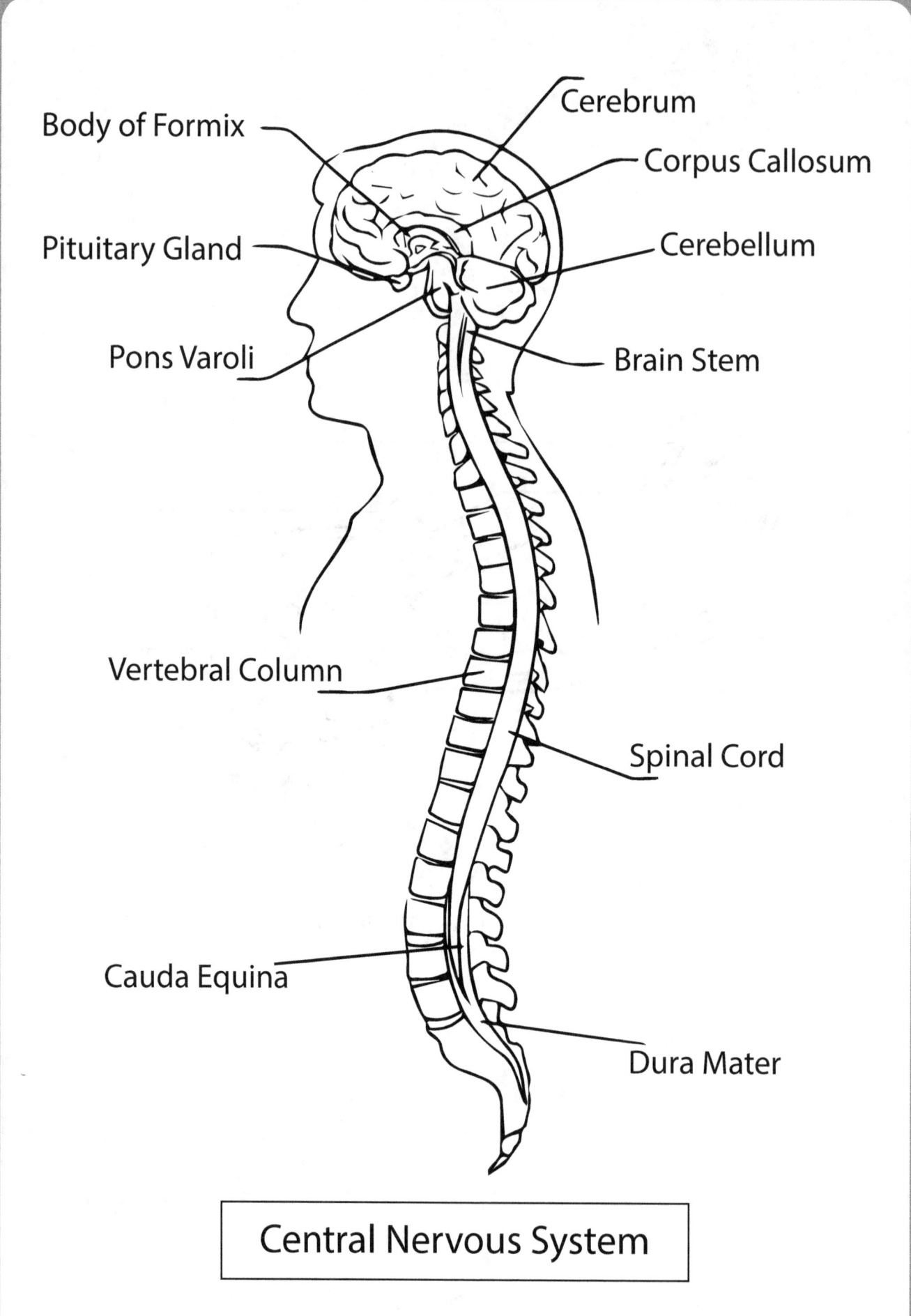

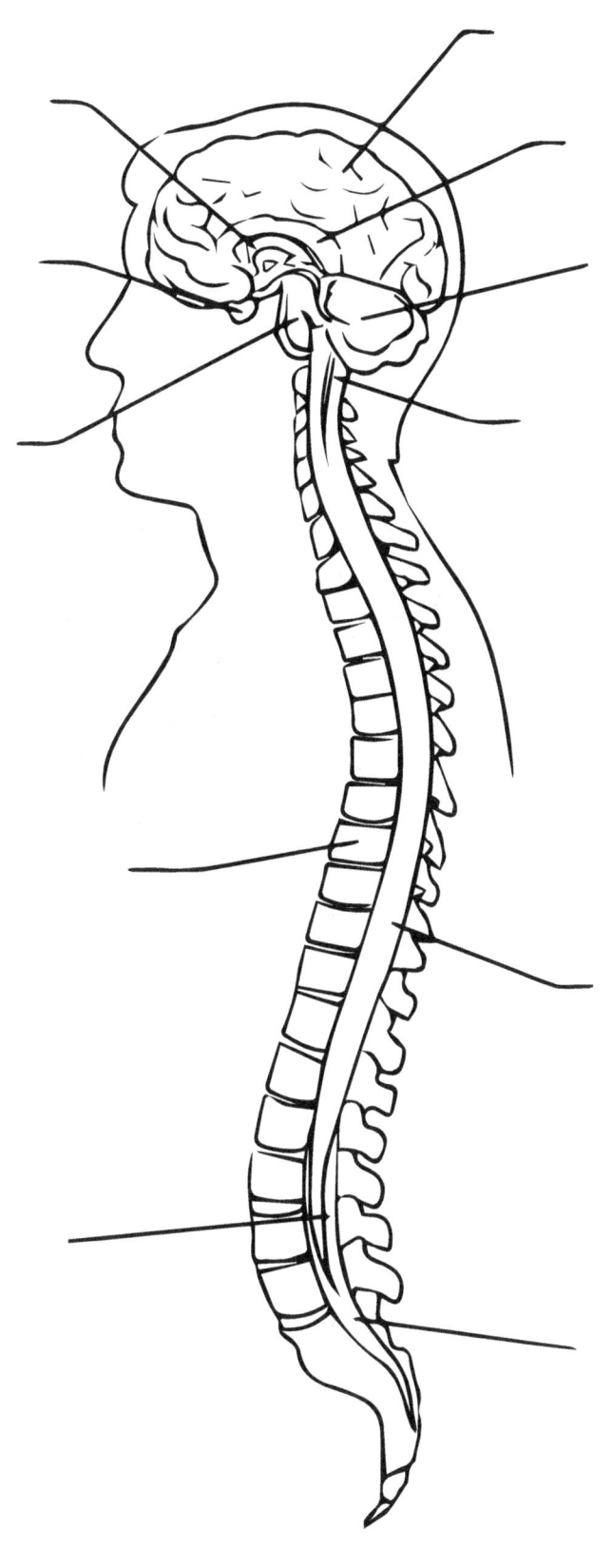

Central Nervous System

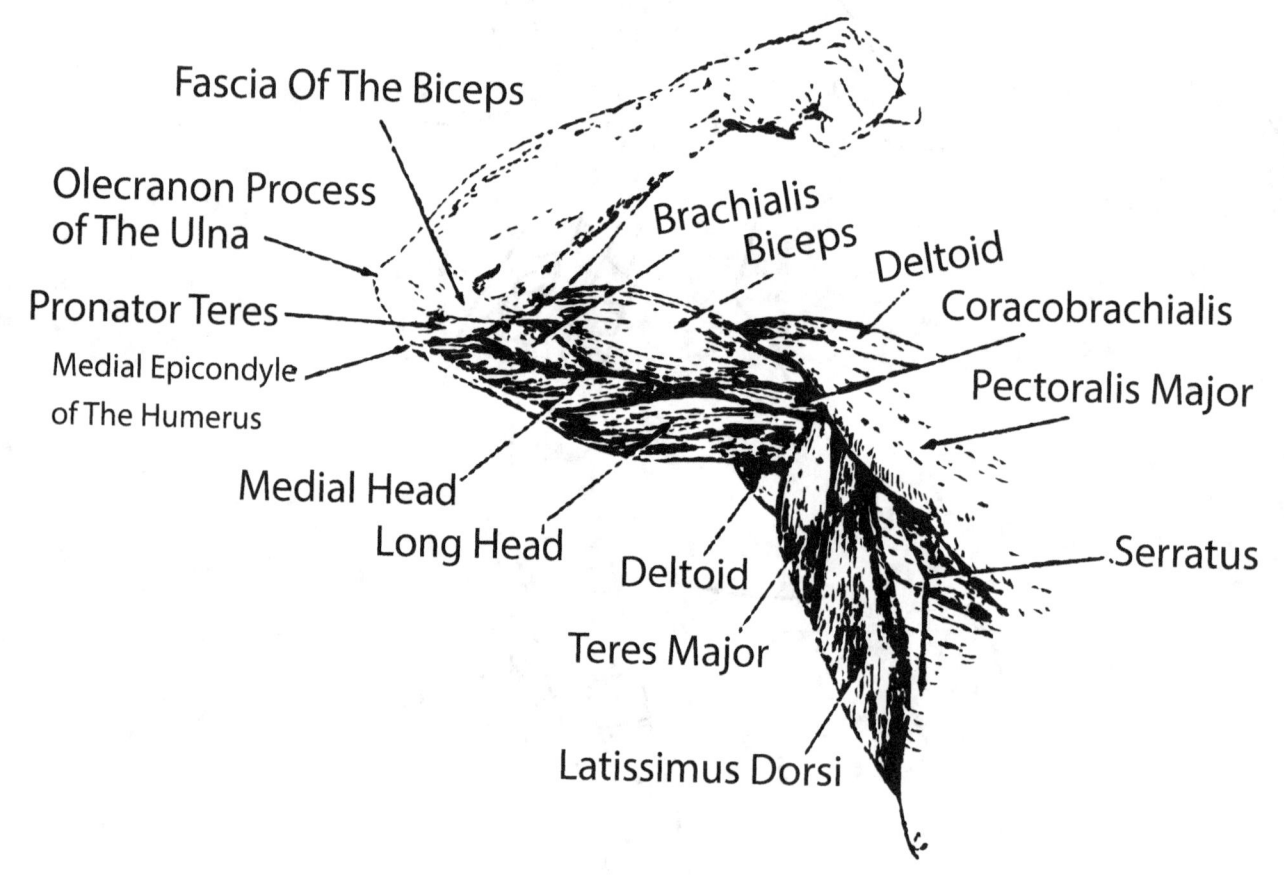

The Muscles

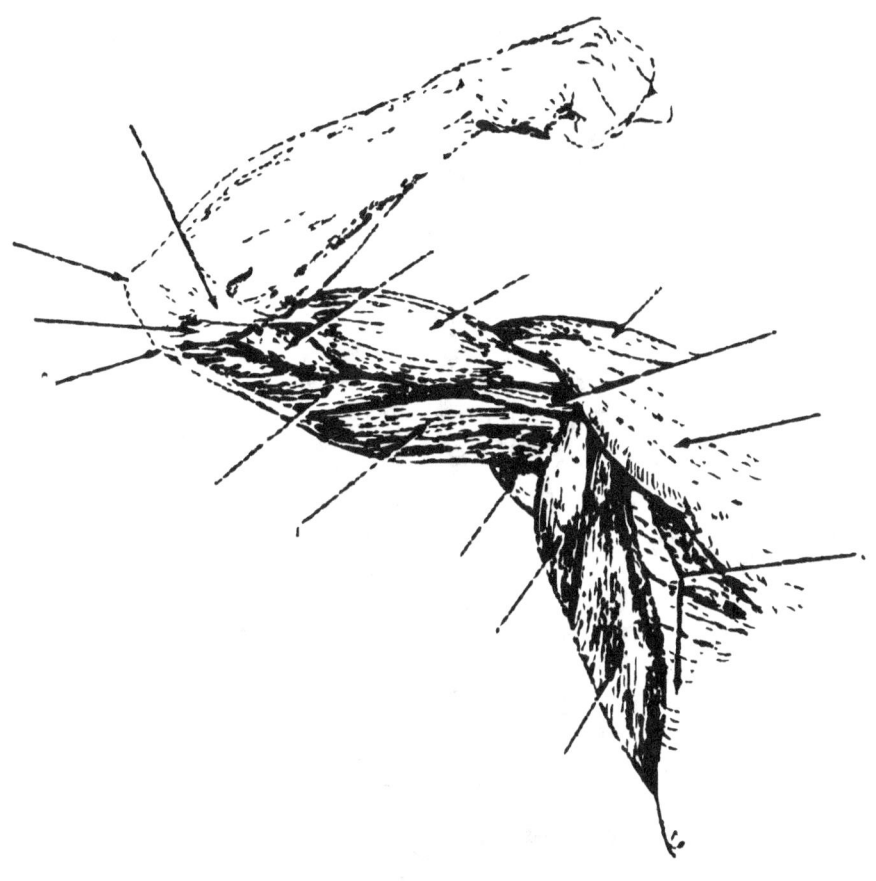

The Muscles

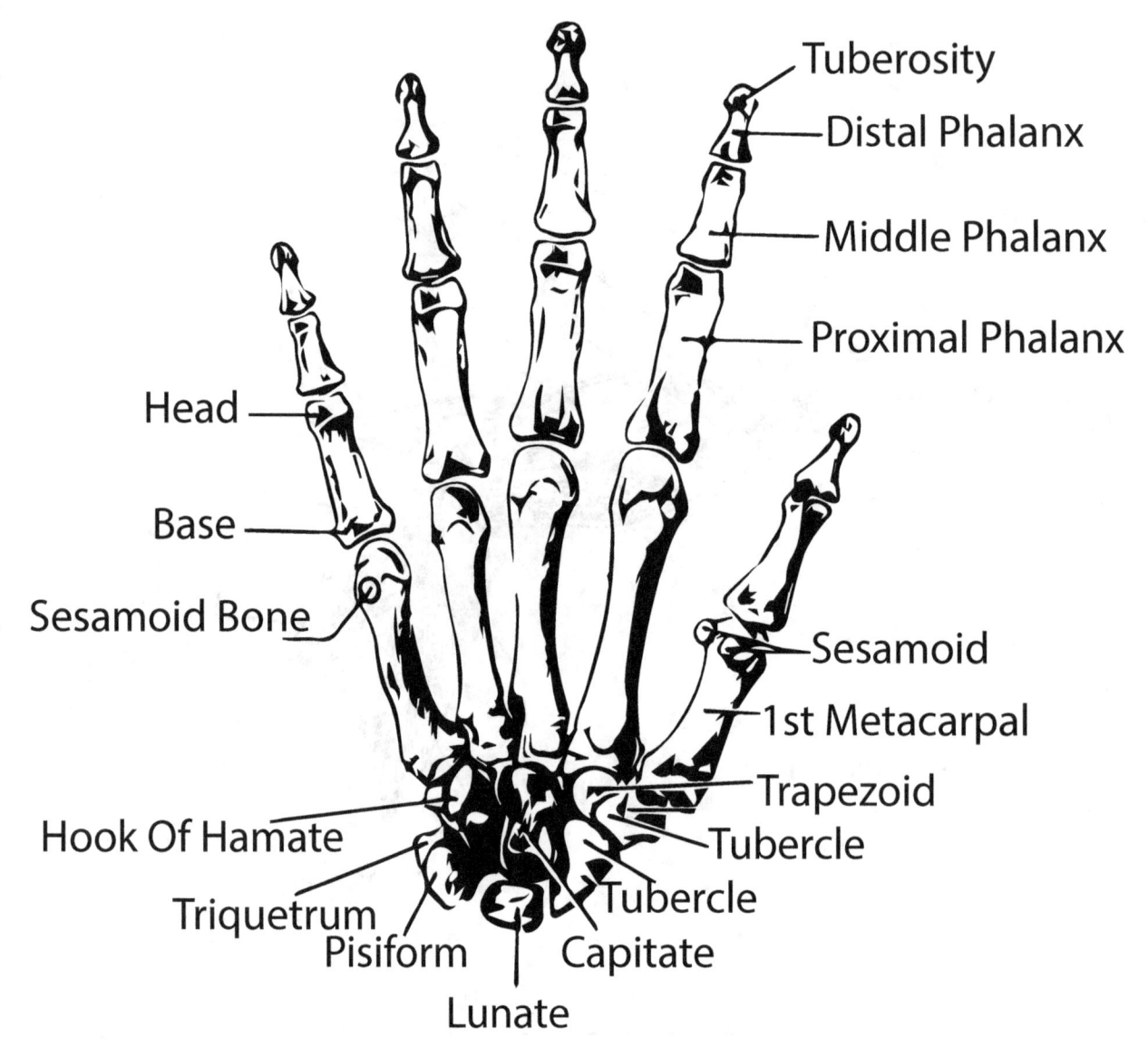

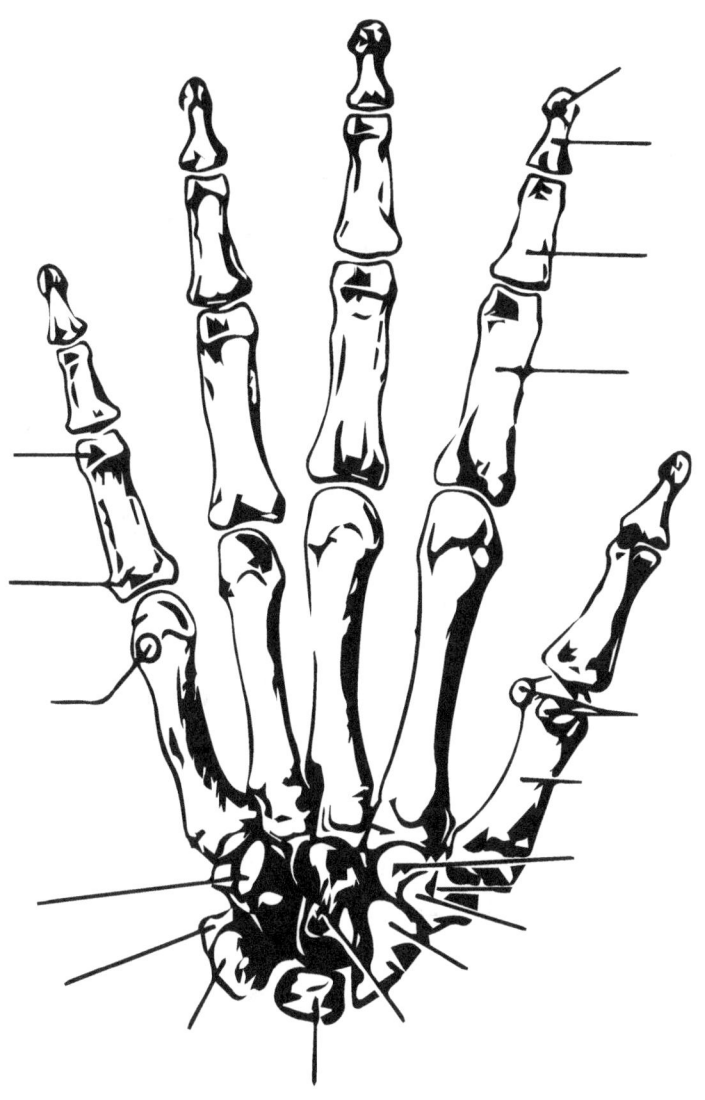

The Hand

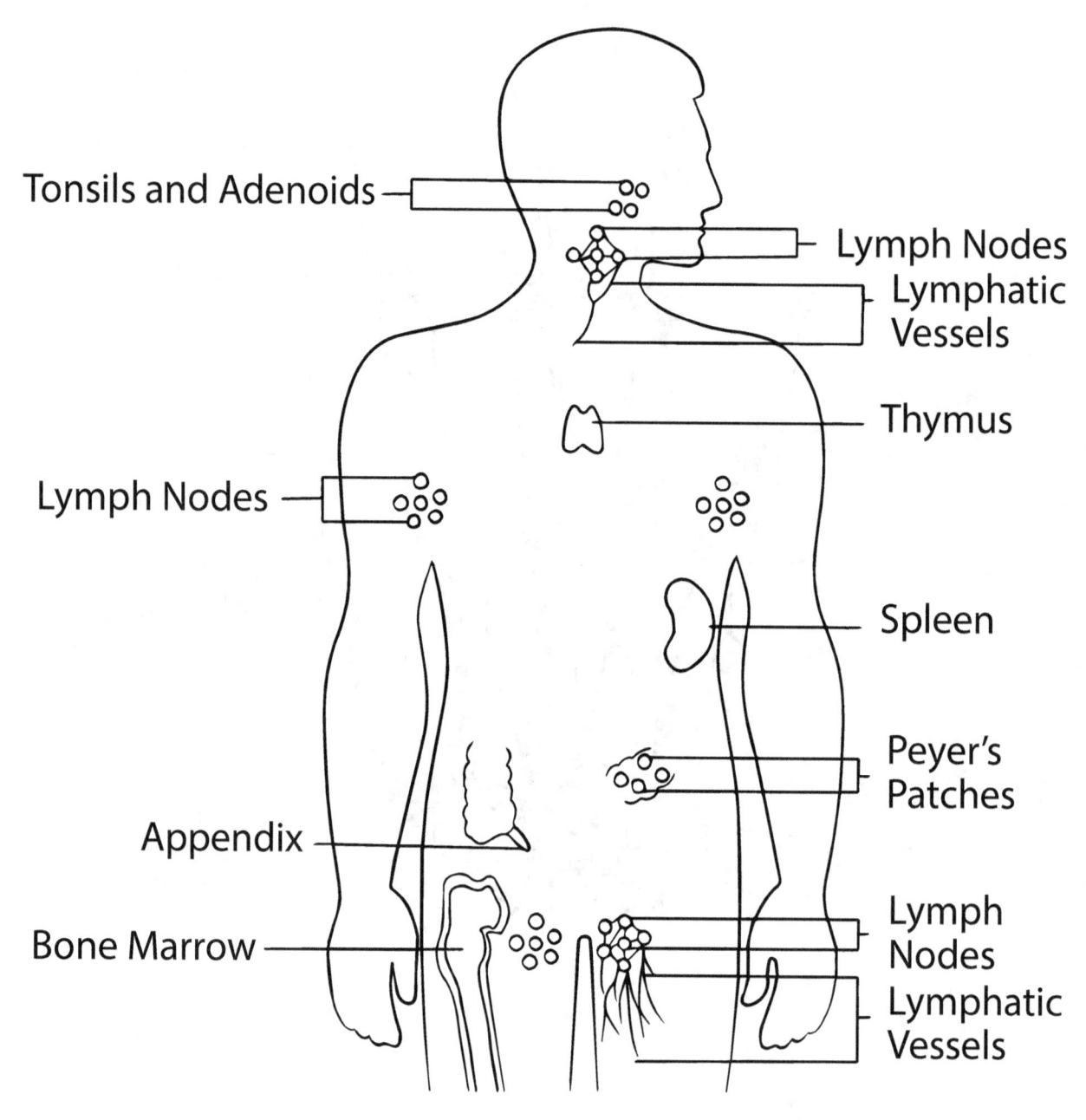

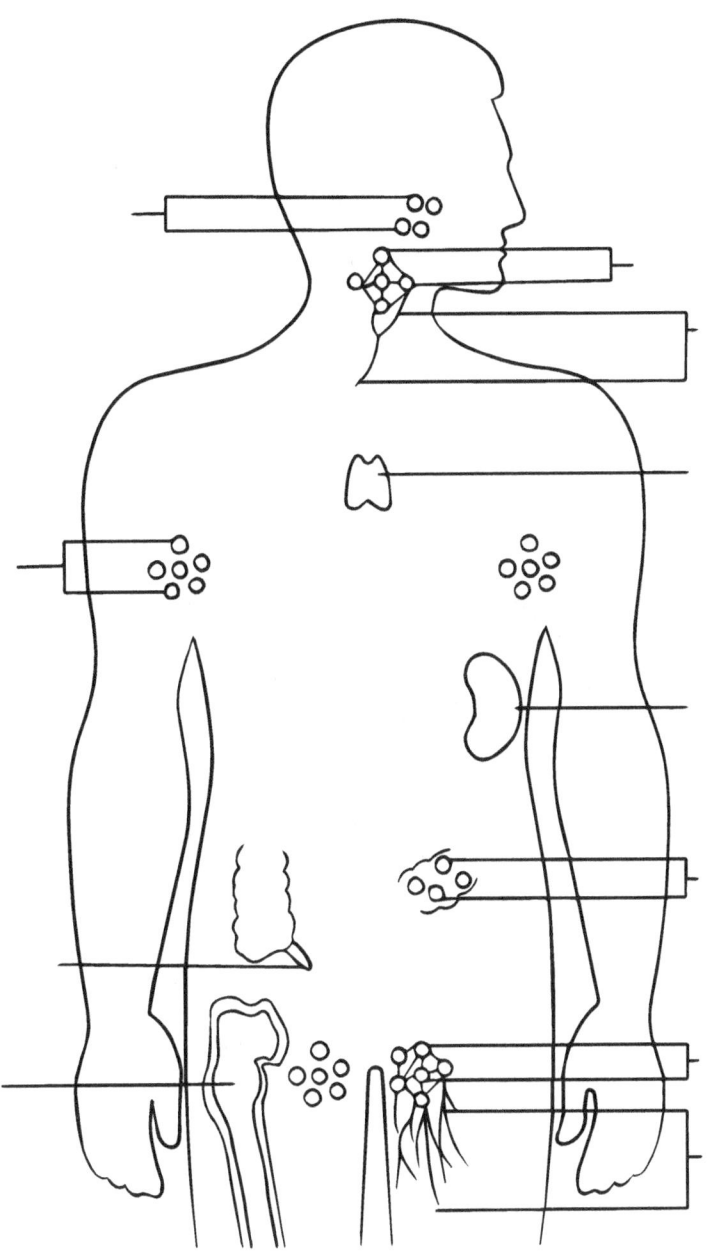

Human Immune System

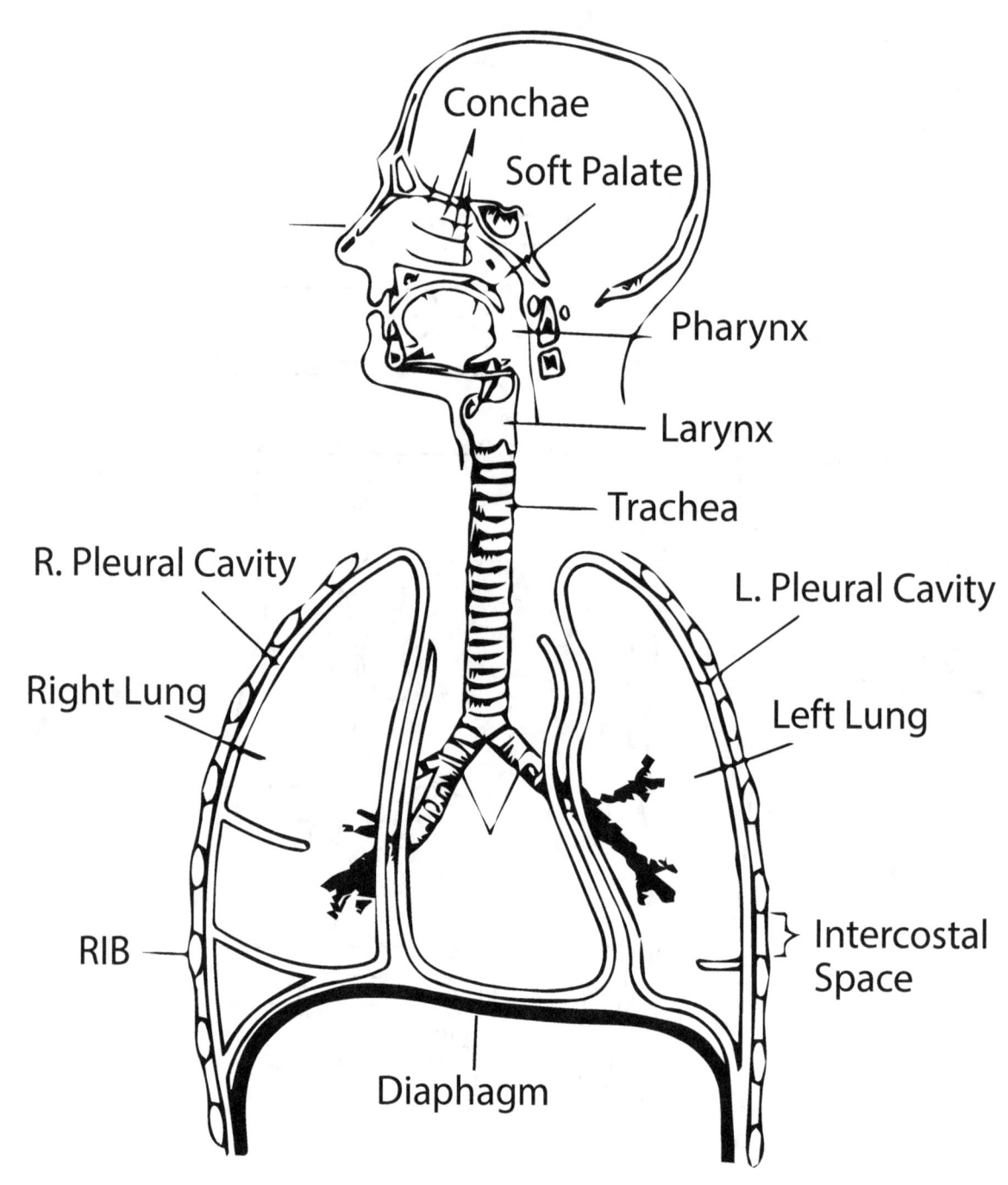

The Lung

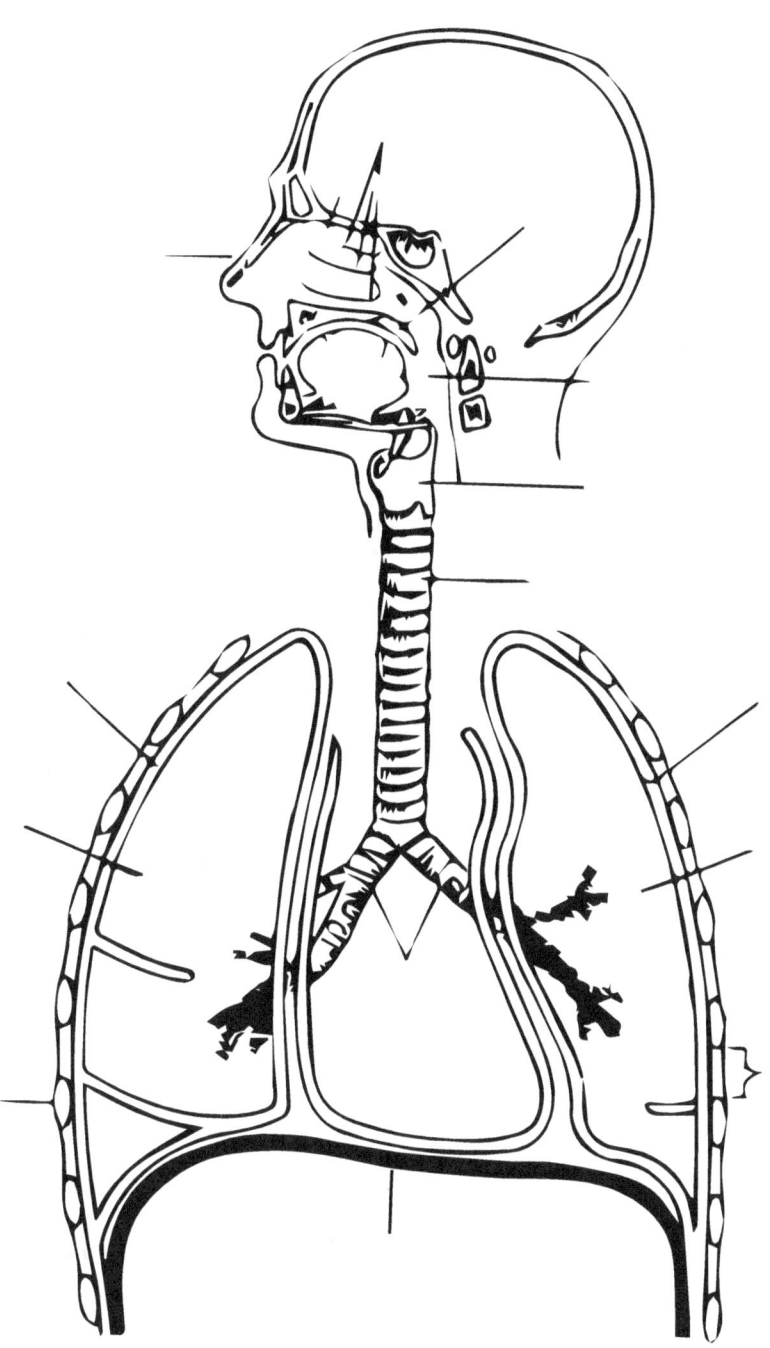

The Lung

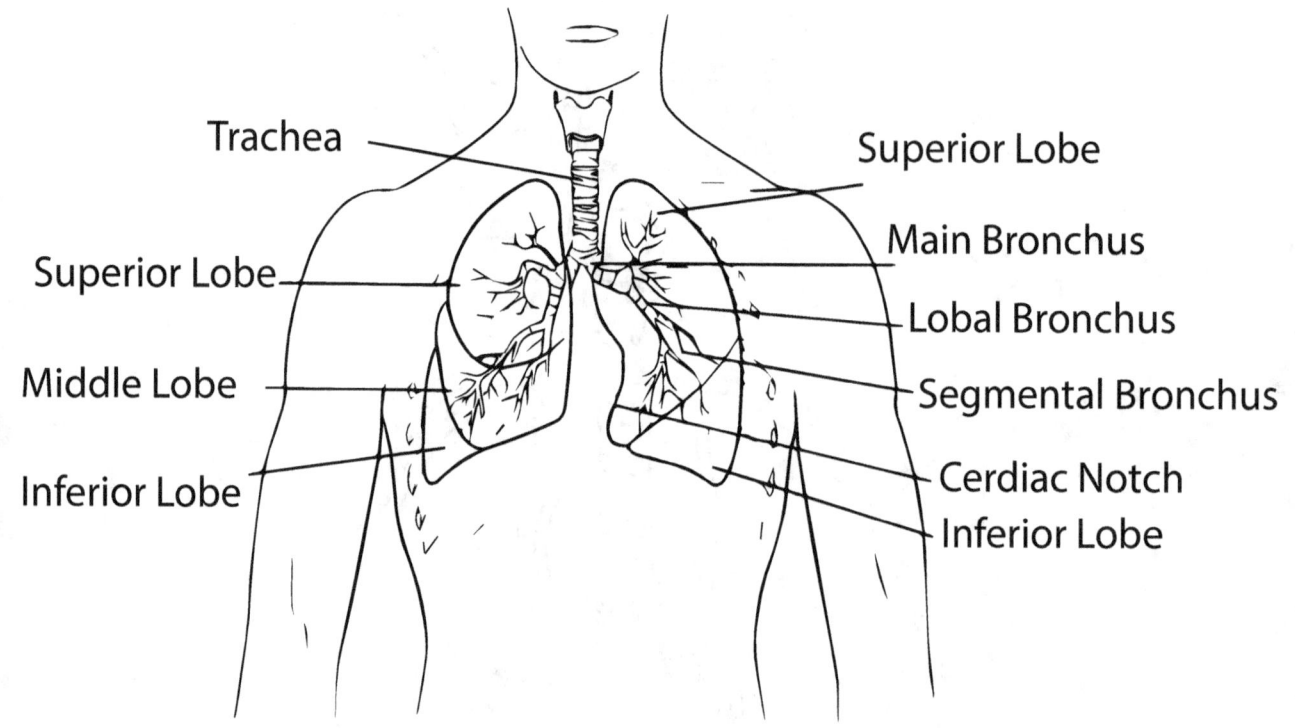

Anatomy Of The Human Lung

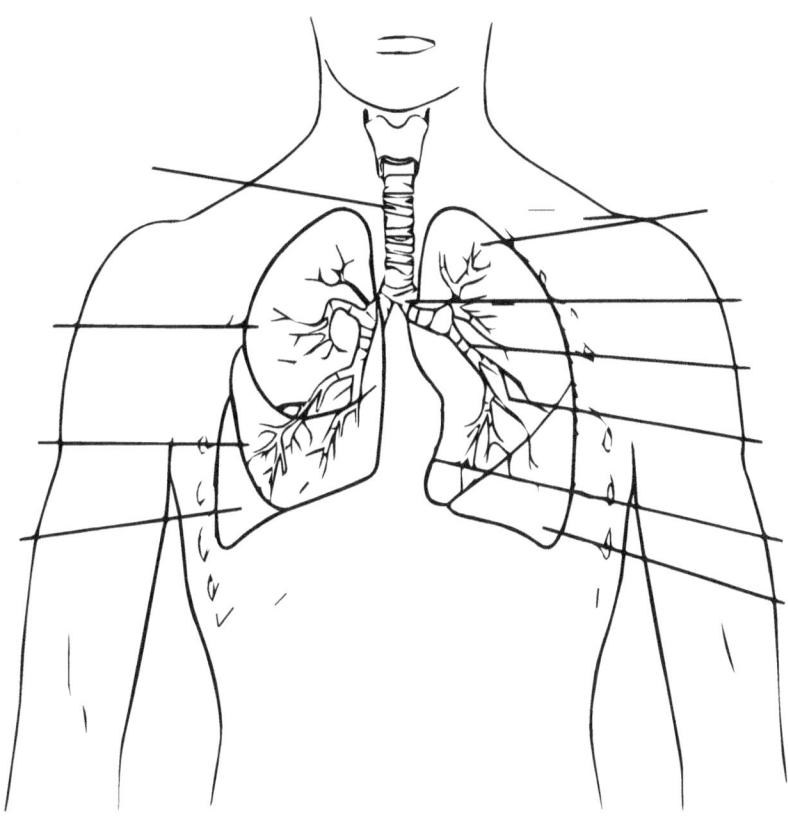

Anatomy Of The Human Lung

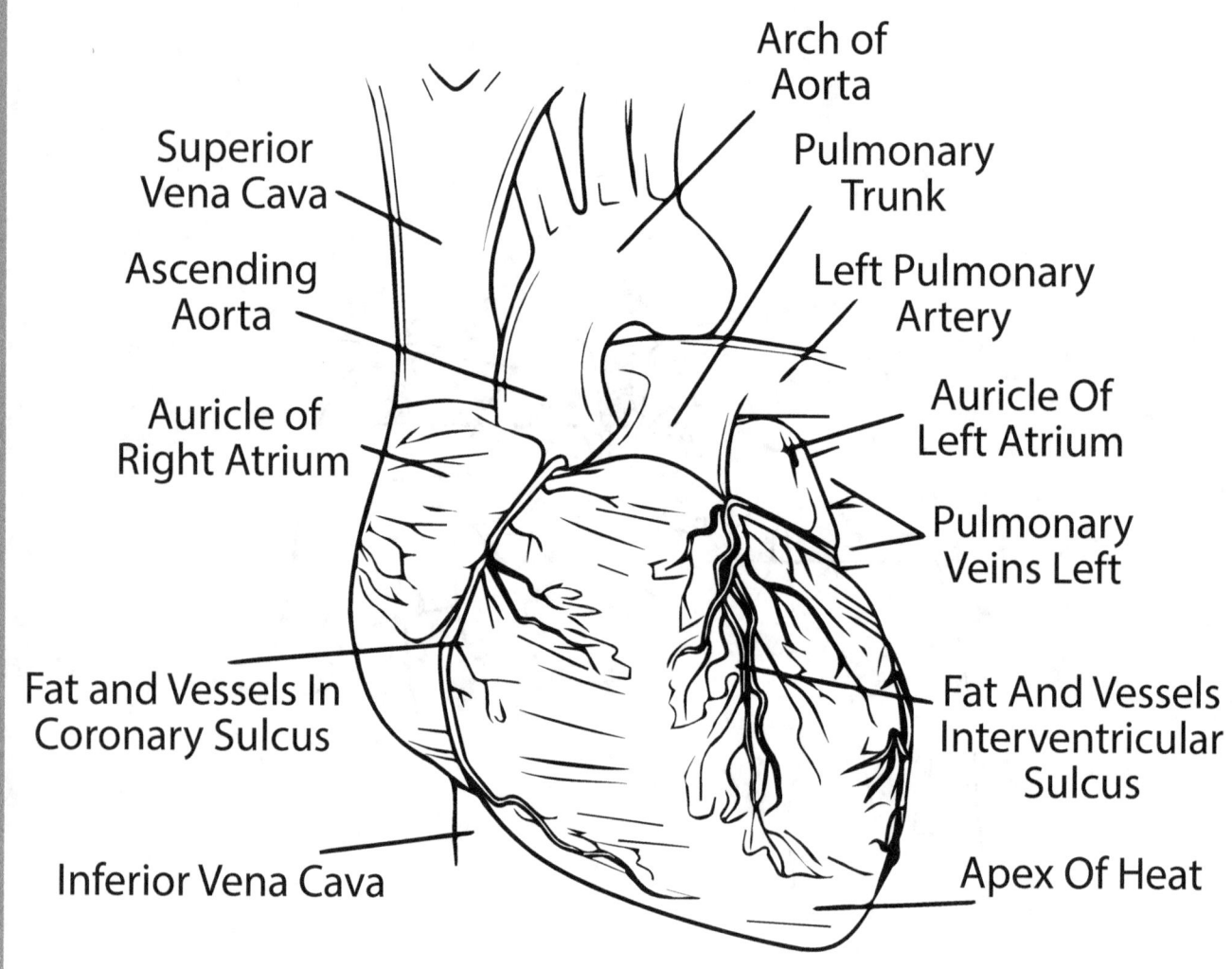

Superficial Heart Anatomy

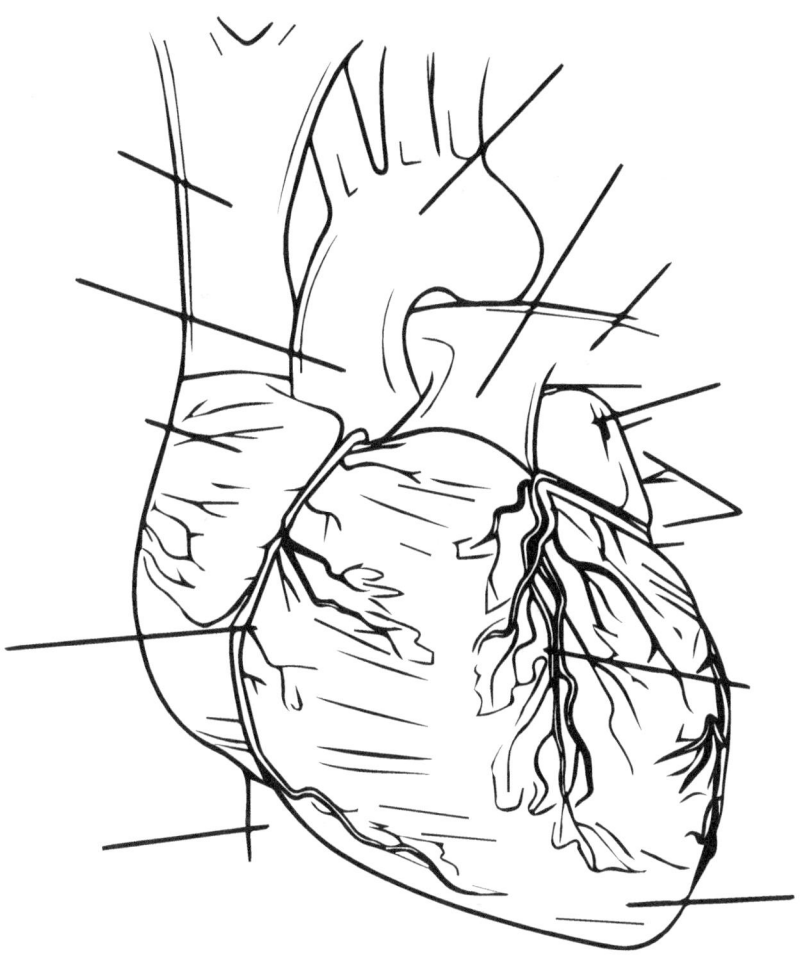

Superficial Heart Anatomy

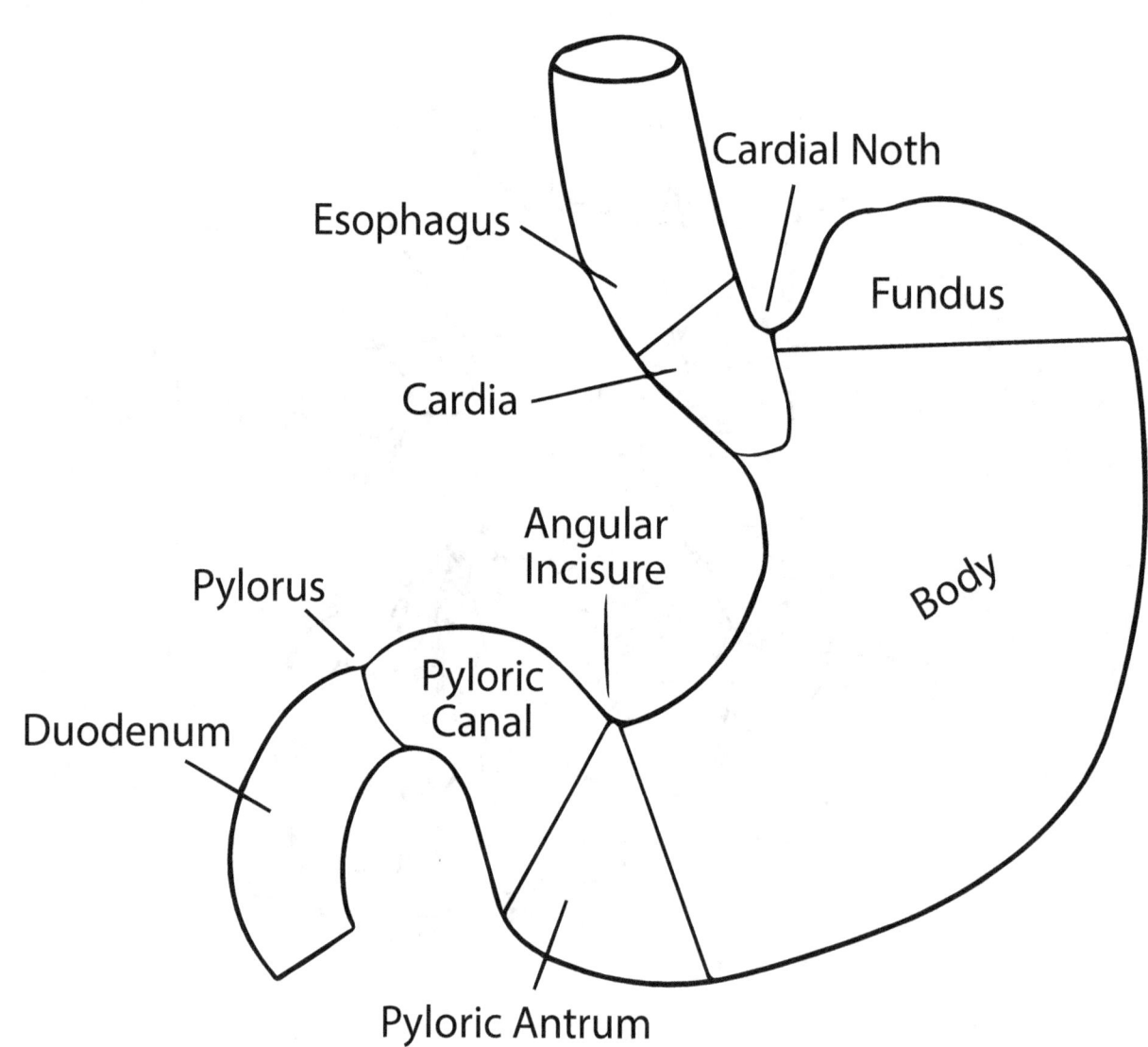

Human Stomach

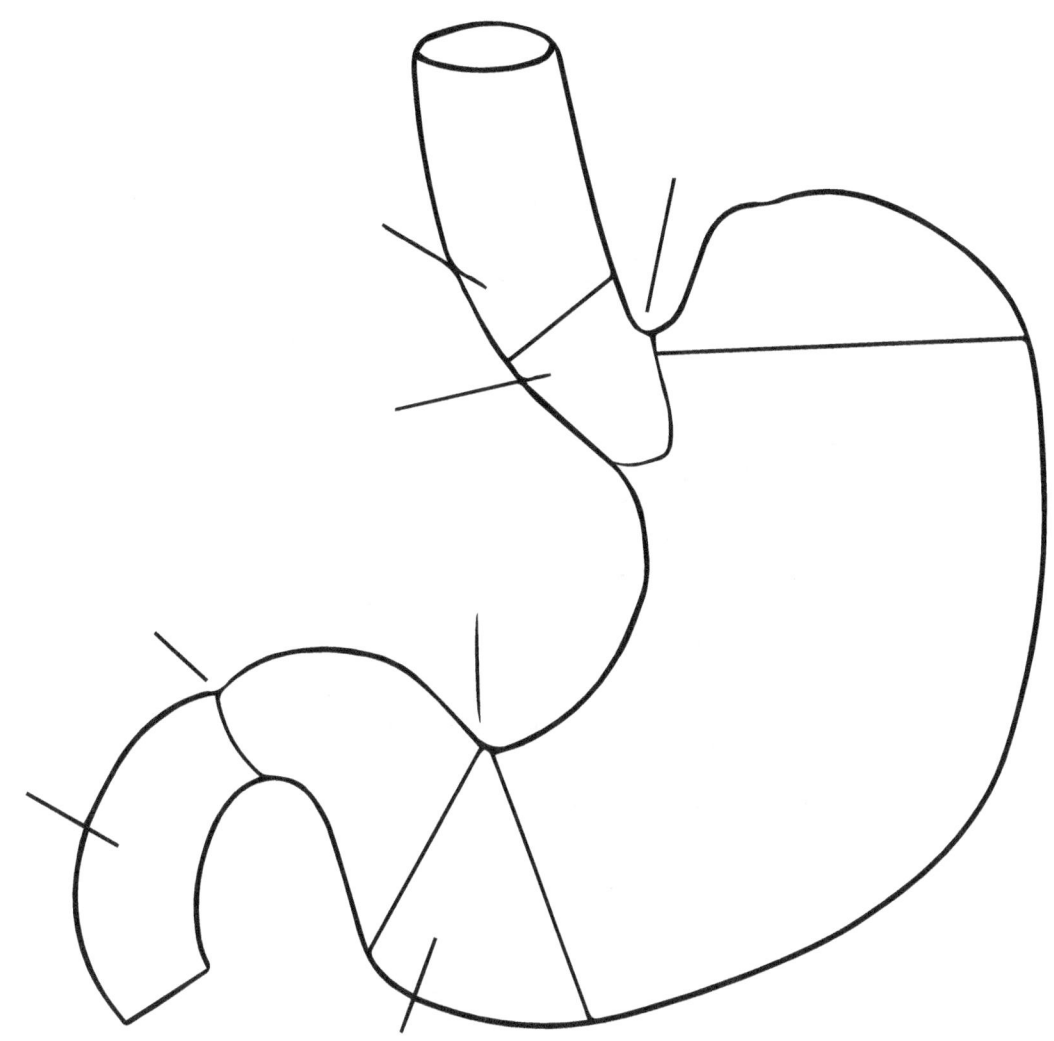

Human Stomach

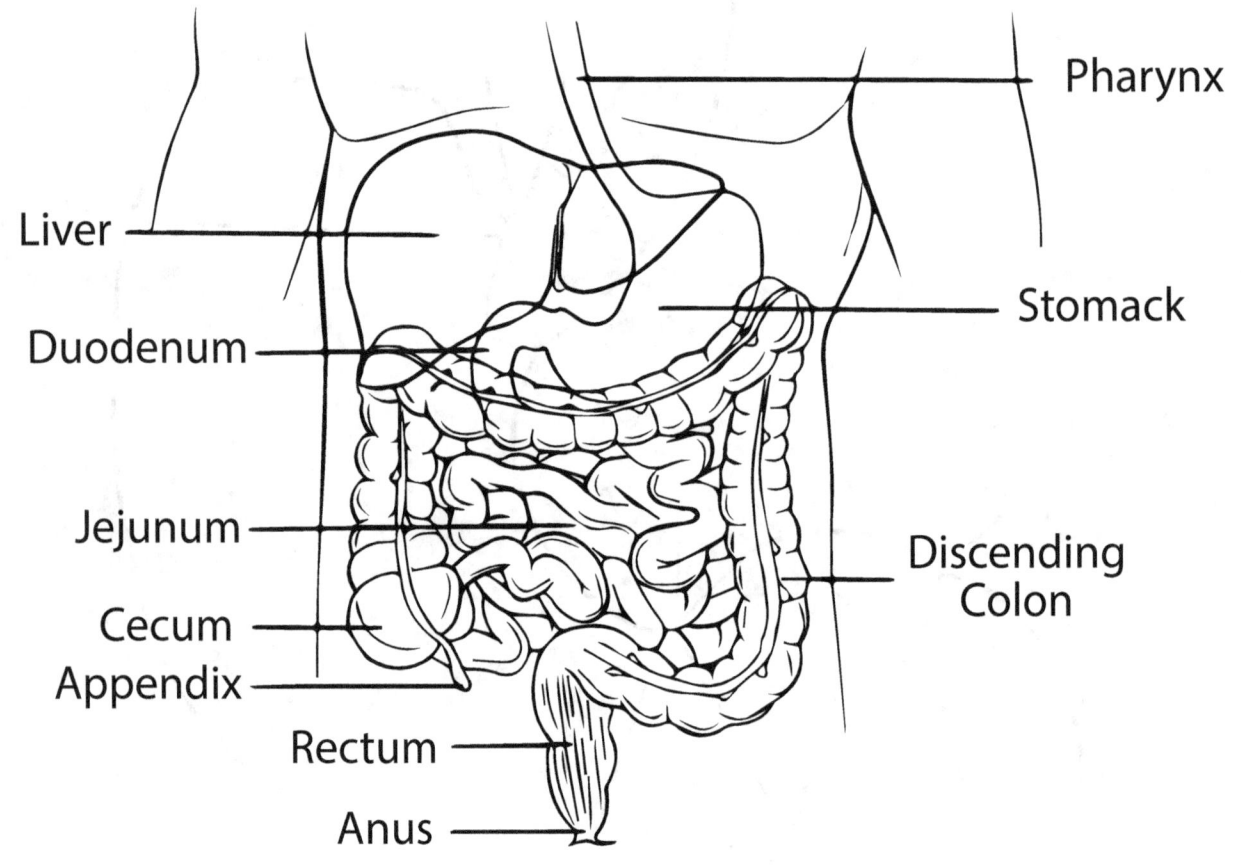

Components of The Digestive System

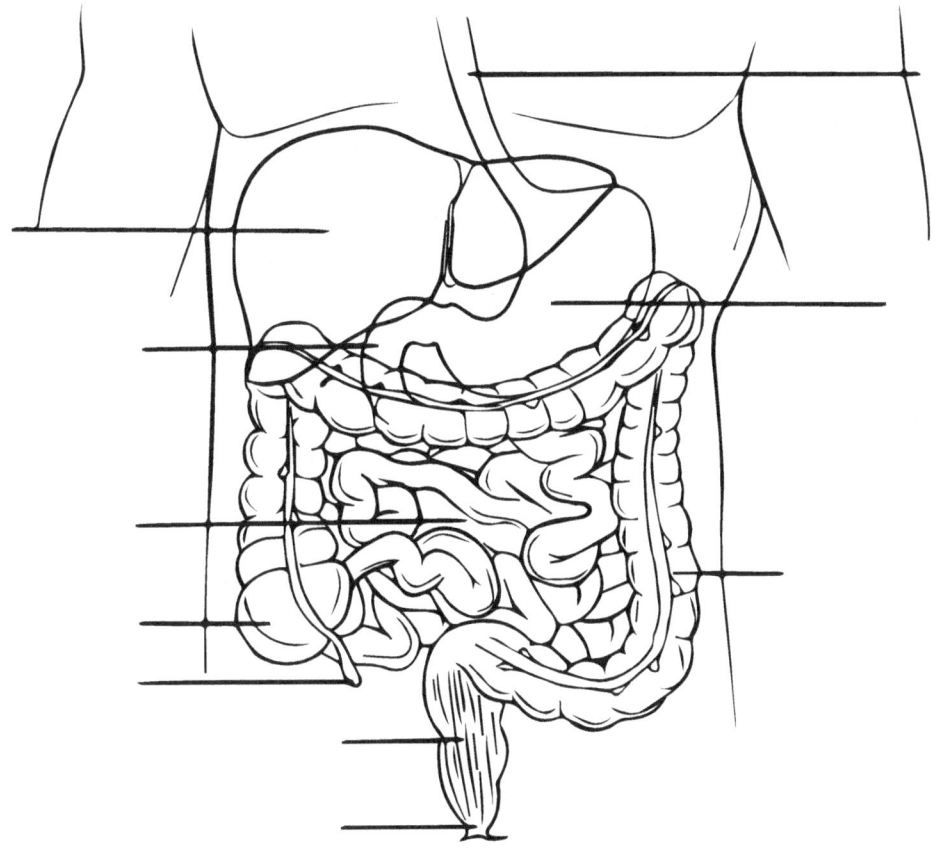

Components of The Digestive System

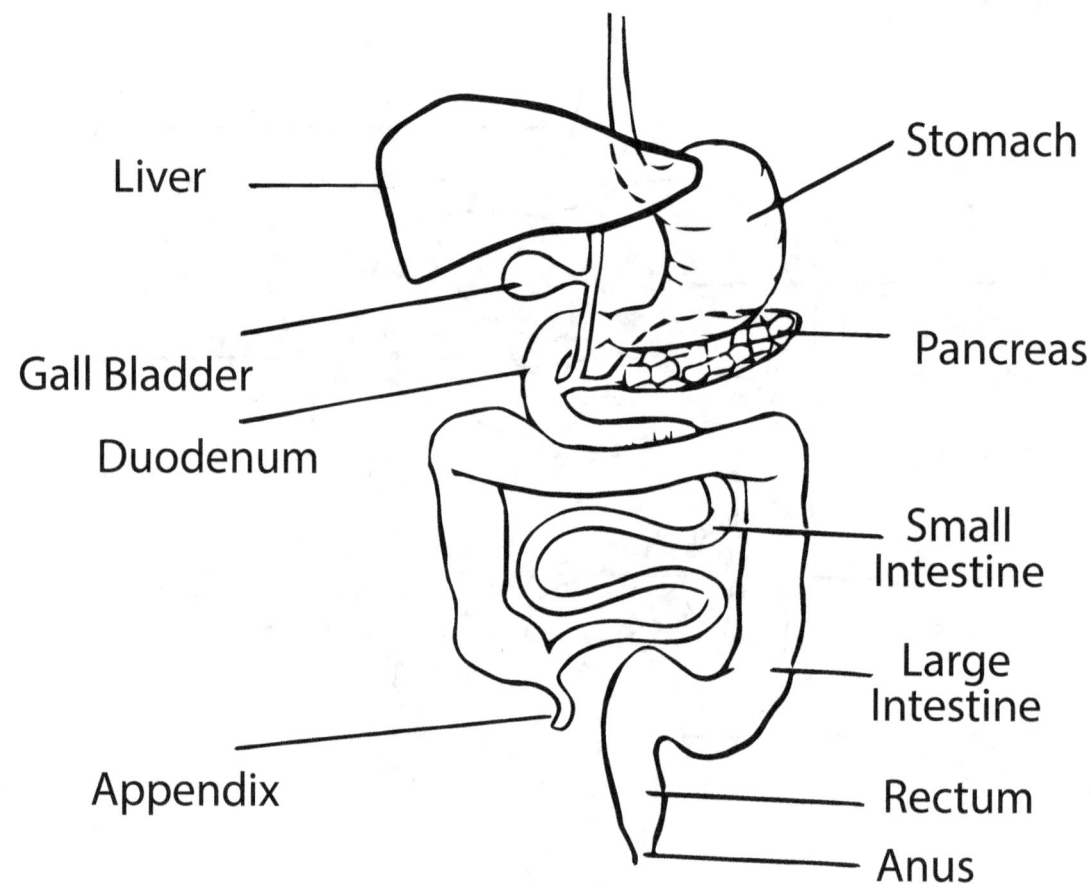

Stomach Working Process

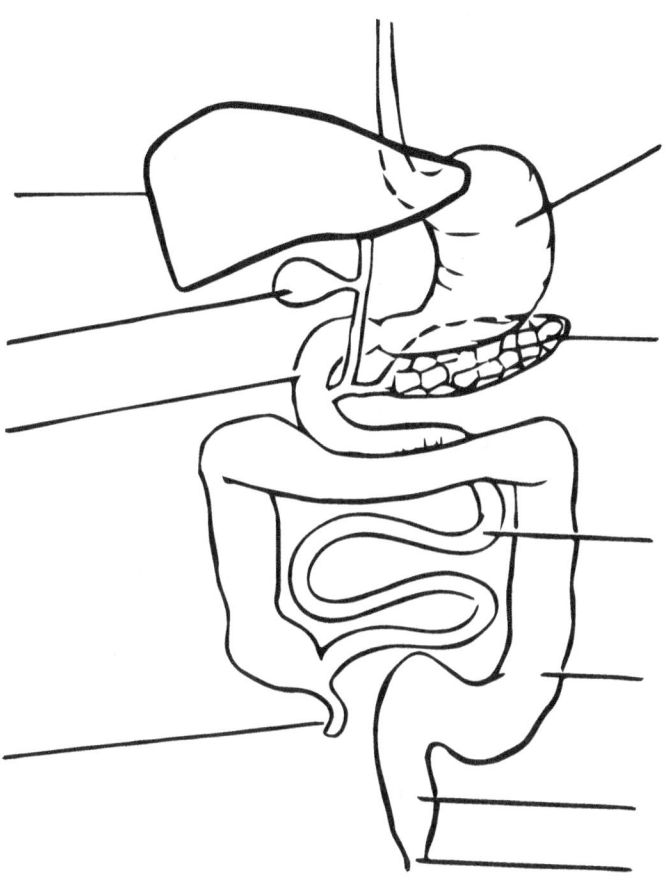

Stomach Working Process

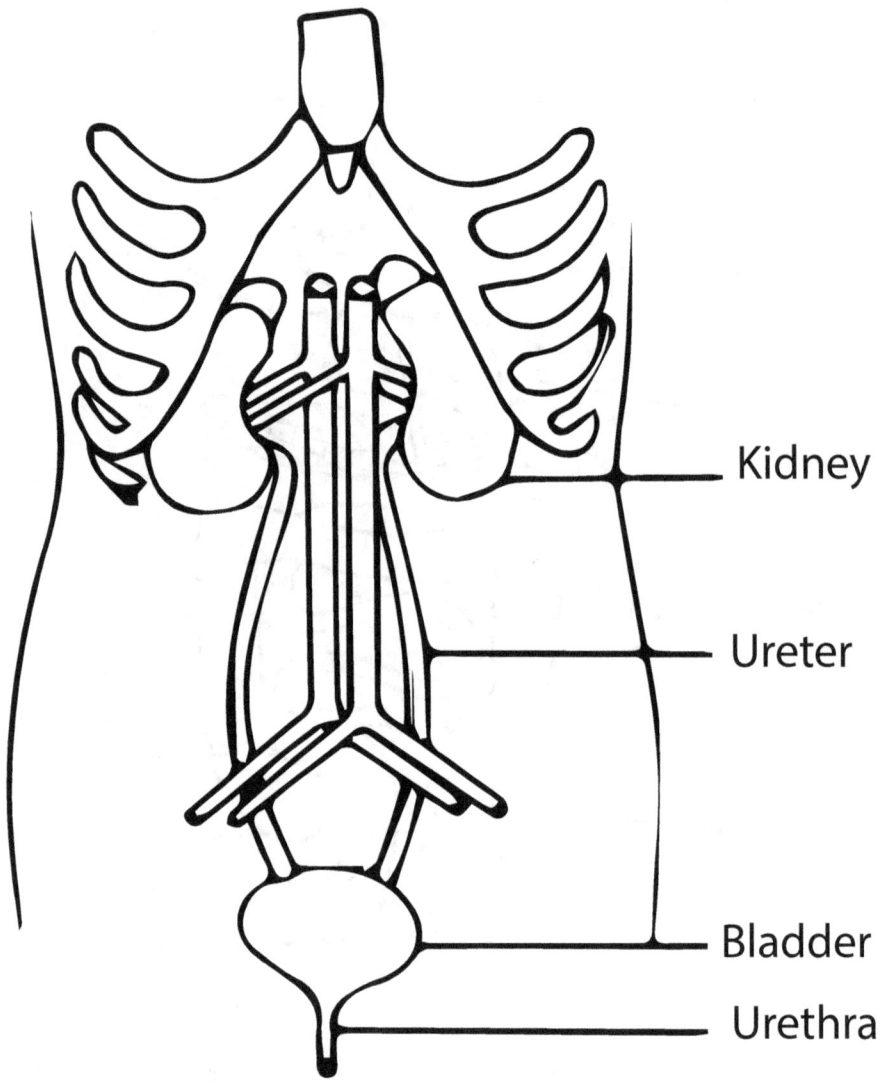

Urinary System

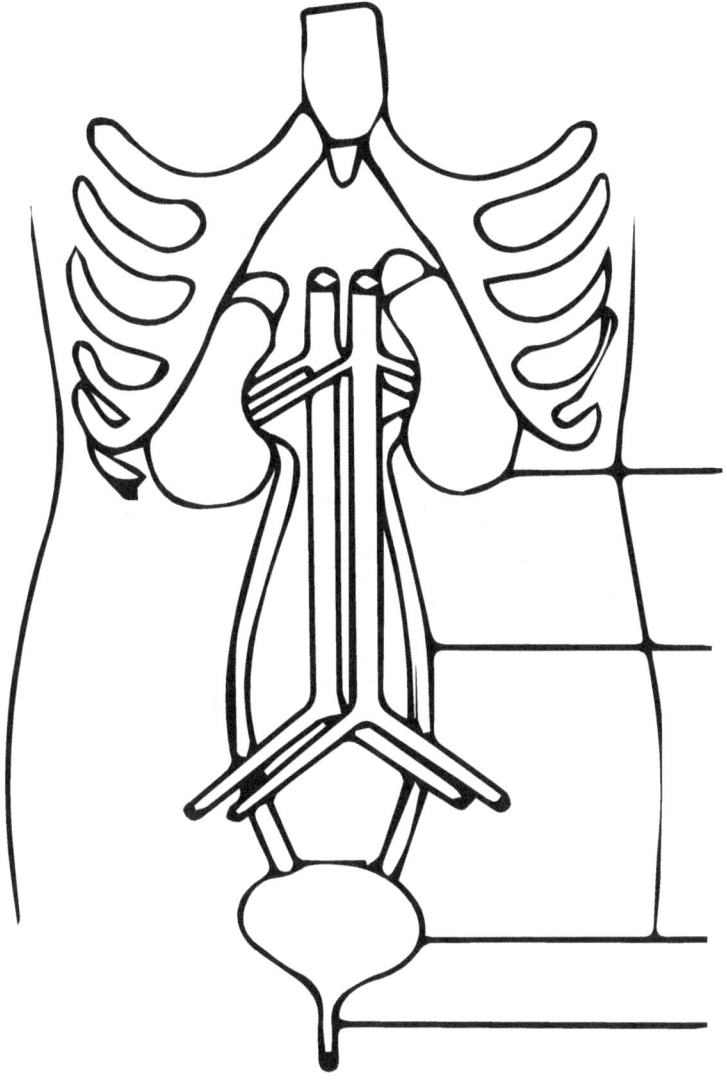

Urinary System

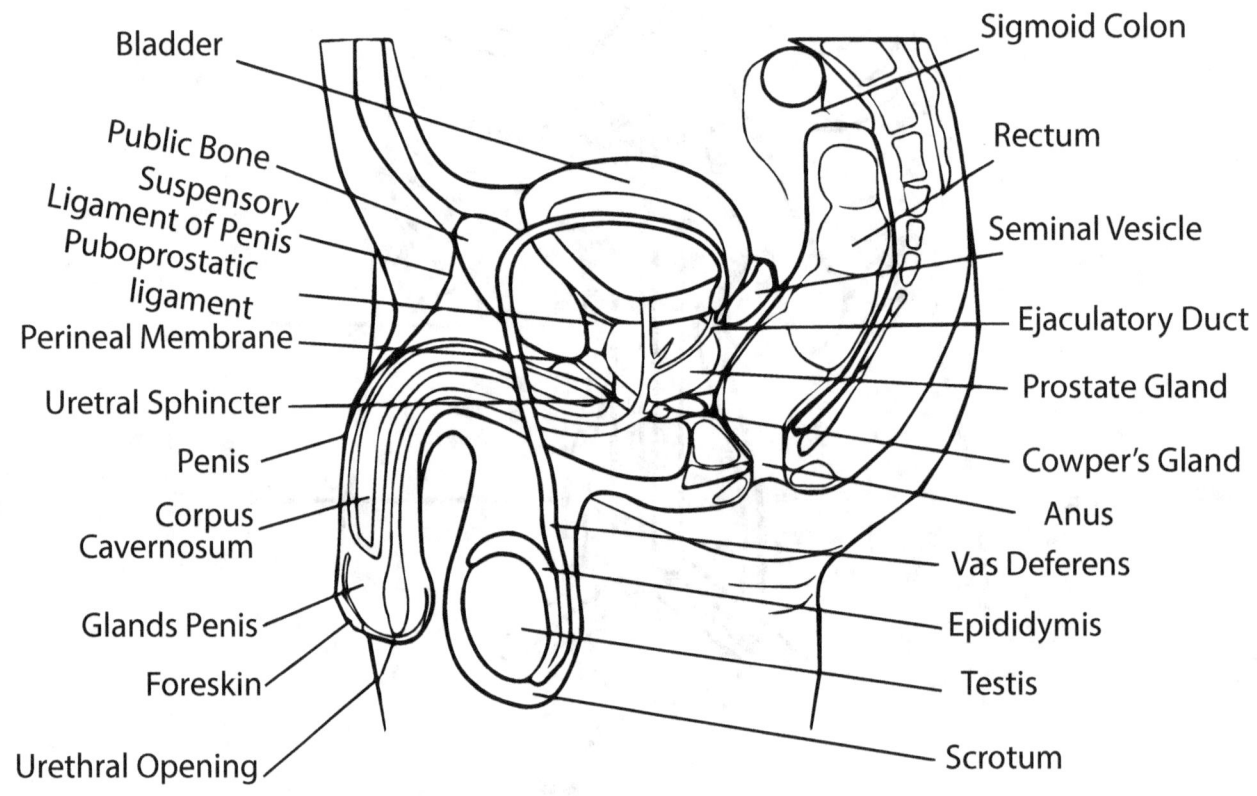

Male Reproductive System

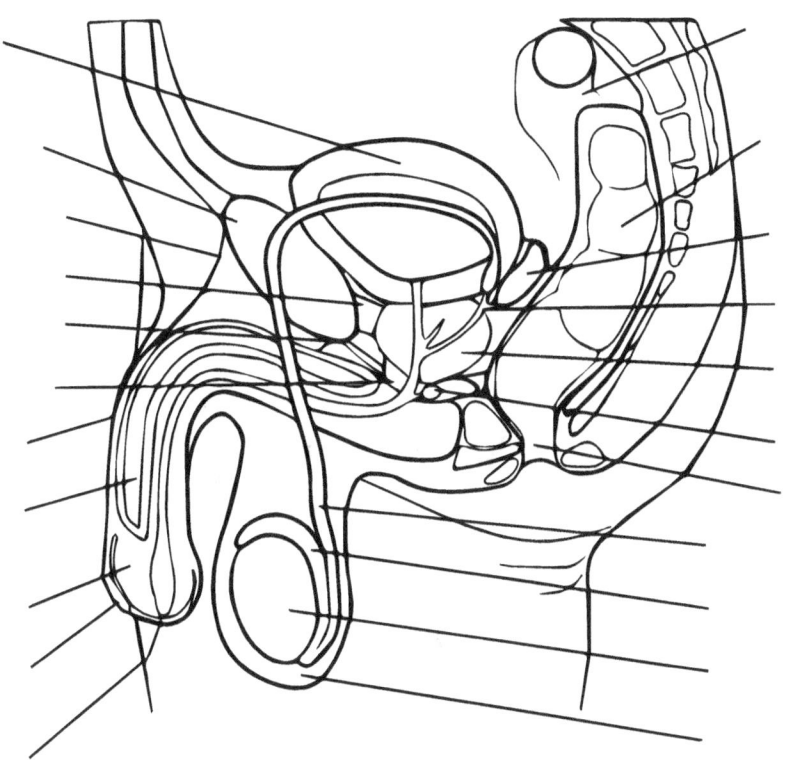

Male Reproductive System

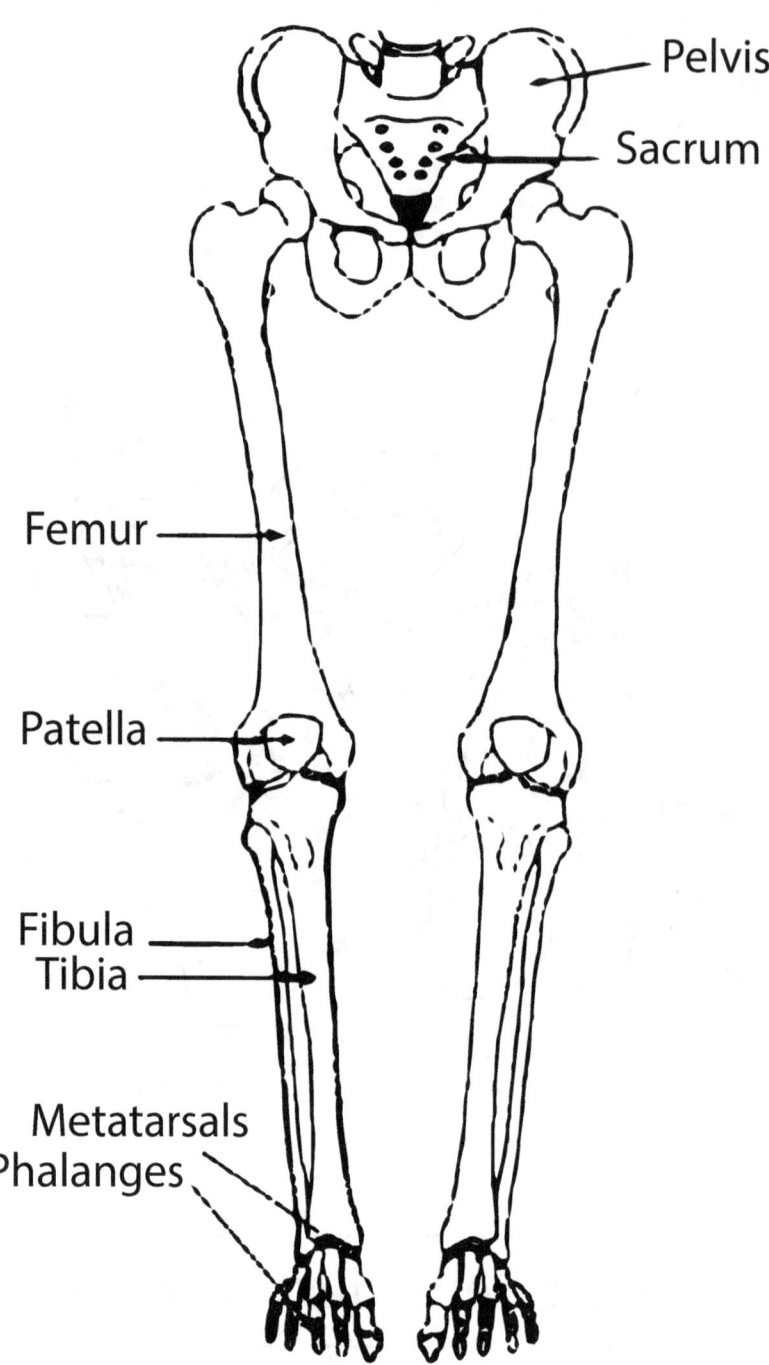

Bones Of The Lower Limb

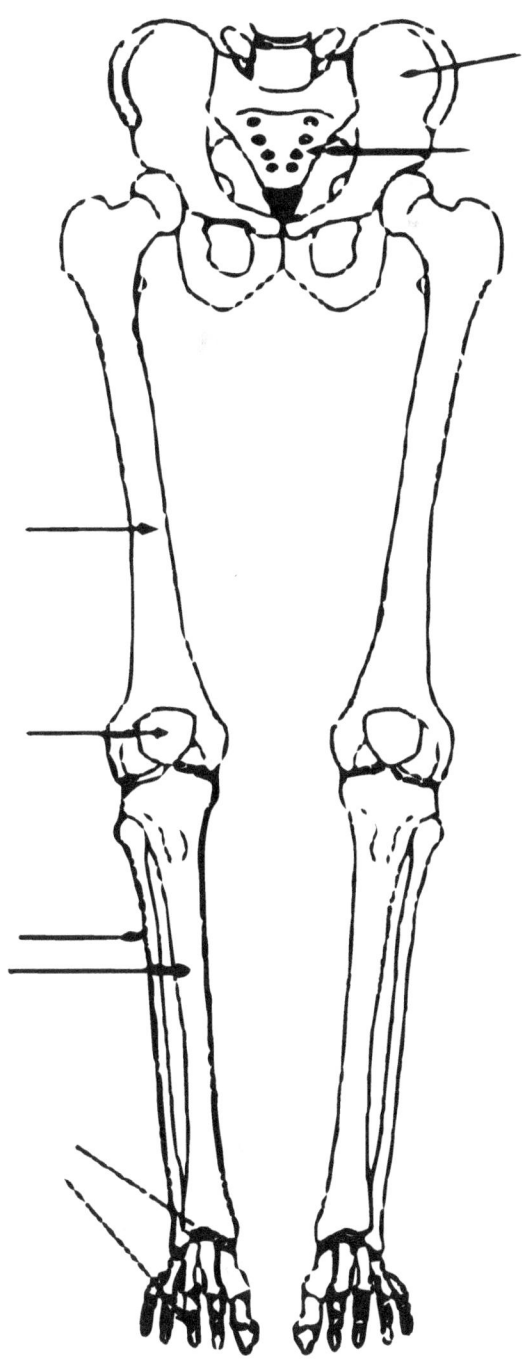

Bones Of The Lower Limb

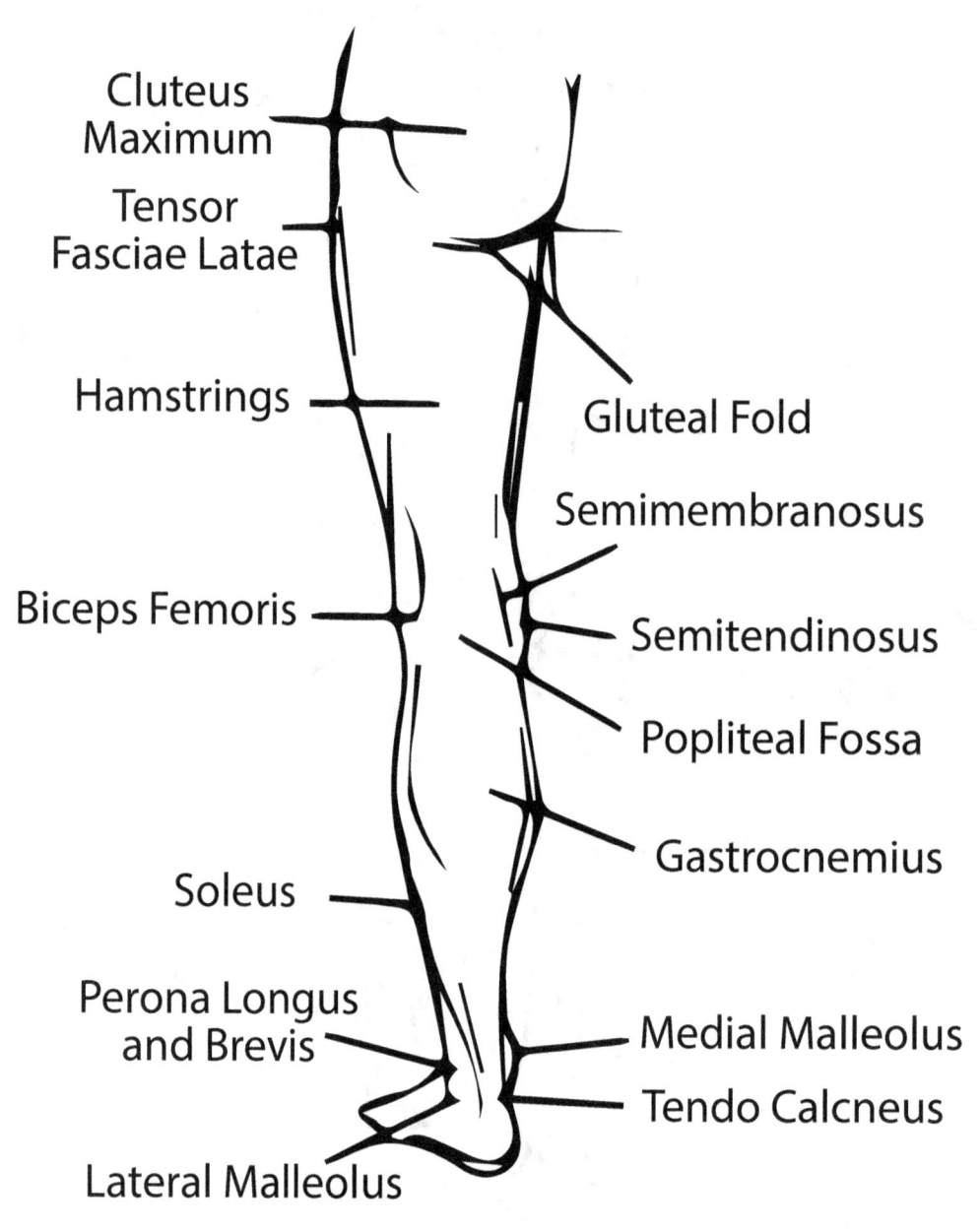

Leg

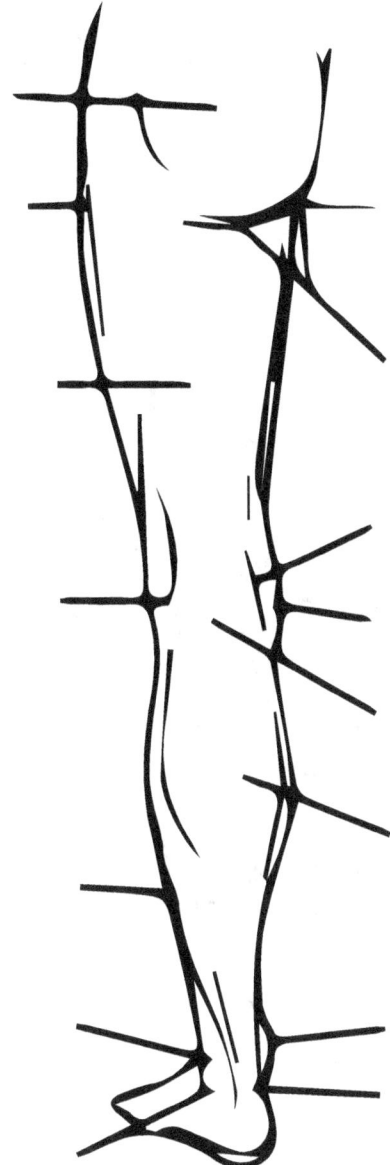

Leg

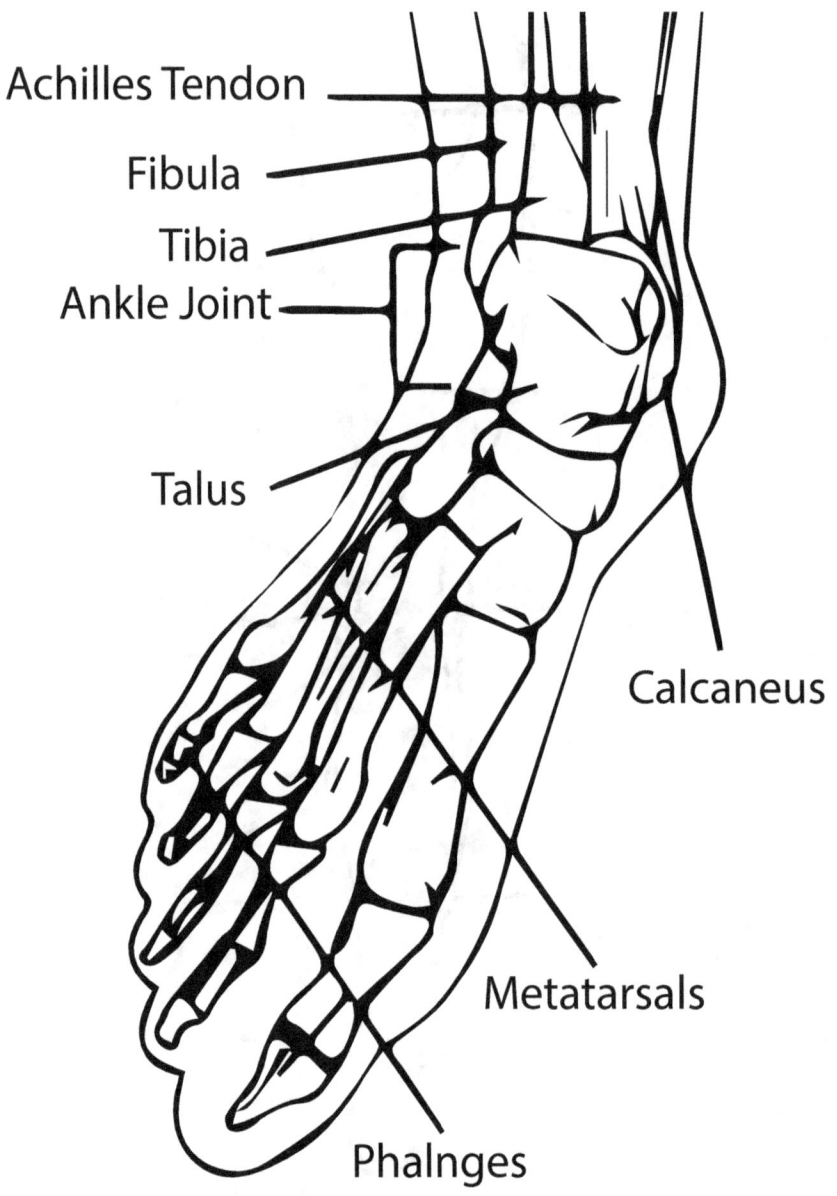

Leg and Foot Lower

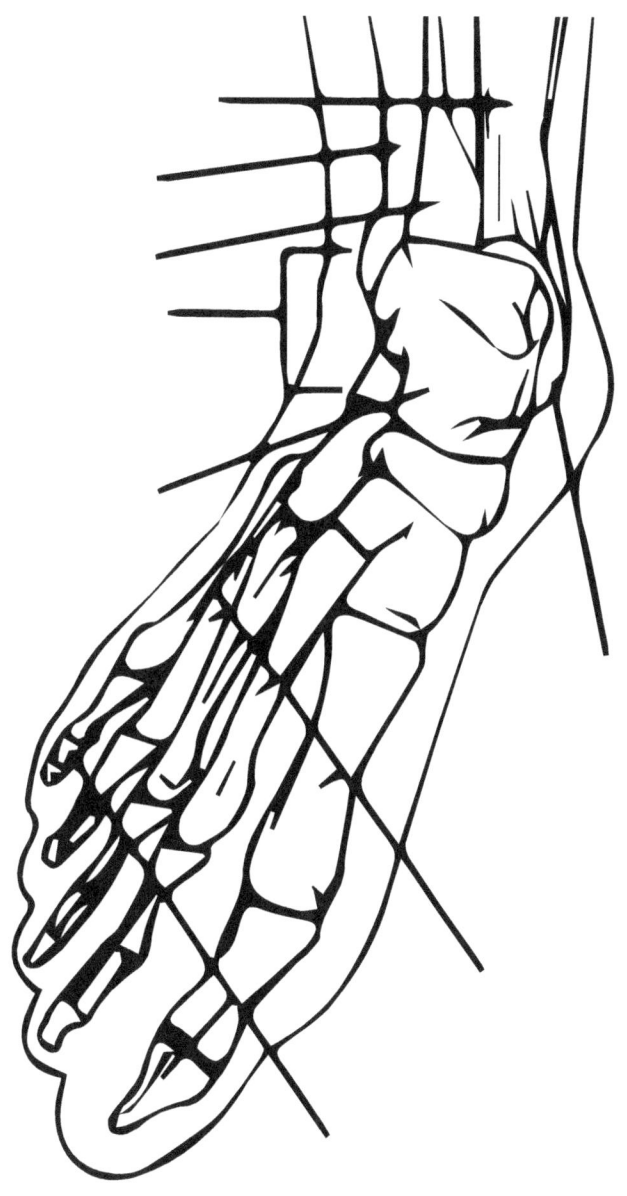

Leg and Foot Lower